.CV

ESSENTIAL CHEMISTRY

STATES
OF MATTER

ESSENTIAL CHEMISTRY

Atoms, Molecules, and Compounds

Chemical Reactions

Metals

The Periodic Table

States of Matter

ESSENTIAL CHEMISTRY

STATES OF MATTER

GASES, LIQUIDS, AND SOLIDS

KRISTA WEST

CHELSEA HOUSE
PUBLISHERS
An imprint of Infobase Publishing

STATES OF MATTER

Chelsea House
An imprint of Infobase Publishing
132 West 31st Street
New York NY 10001

Library of Congress Cataloging-in-Publication Data

West, Krista.
  States of matter / Krista West.
    p. cm. — (Essential chemistry)
  Includes bibliographical references and index.
  ISBN 978-0-7910-9521-8 (hardcover)
  1. Matter—Constitution. 2. Matter—Properties. I. Title. II. Series.

  QC173.W452 2007
  530.4—dc22   2007047568

Chelsea House books are available at special discounts when purchased in bulk quantities for businesses, associations, institutions, or sales promotions. Please call our Special Sales Department in New York at (212) 967-8800 or (800) 322-8755.

You can find Chelsea House on the World Wide Web at http://www.chelseahouse.com

Series design by Erik Lindstrom
Cover design by Ben Peterson

Printed in the United States of America

Bang NMSG 10 9 8 7 6 5 4 3 2 1

This book is printed on acid-free paper.

All links and Web addresses were checked and verified to be correct at the time of publication. Because of the dynamic nature of the Web, some addresses and links may have changed since publication and may no longer be valid.

CONTENTS

Nature's
Matter Mover

A hurricane is one of nature's most powerful forces. It starts nice and easy, slowly picking a path across warm ocean waters and gathering its strength. Then with a large rev of its engine, it turns into a powerful force that can change the shape of the land in very little time. To those on land, the force of a hurricane may seem to have little purpose. But step back for a moment and you see that hurricanes are one of nature's best matter movers.

Hurricanes turn warm ocean waters into hot, humid air; then they turn that air into rain that can soak a city or create unexpected snowstorms in August. Hurricanes change the form, or state, of water and move it across the surface of our planet.

But hurricanes are not the only forces that move water around the globe. In fact, water is constantly in motion on the planet as part of Earth's water cycle. The **water cycle** describes the movement of water at, above, and below the surface of the Earth.

To move water at the surface of the Earth, the water cycle uses phase changes. A **phase change** occurs when matter changes its form, or state. This includes instances when a substance changes from liquid to gas (or gas to liquid), liquid to solid (or solid to liquid), or solid to gas (or gas to solid).

Arguably, there is nowhere on Earth where phase changes are more natural and more important than in Earth's water cycle. These processes keep the balance of water fairly constant in our oceans,

HURRICANE KATRINA

Hurricanes can be useful to the planet, but they aren't always good for humans. In August 2005, one of the five deadliest hurricanes in U.S. history struck the southeastern part of the country, from Louisiana to Alabama, and virtually destroyed the legendary city of New Orleans.

The hurricane began as a tropical depression on August 23, 2005, near the Bahamas. A tropical depression is characterized by surface winds blowing between 23 and 39 miles (37 and 63 km) per hour. By the next day, the tropical depression was upgraded to a tropical storm, an area with stronger winds and rain. It was given the name *Katrina*. The storm started moving toward the southeast coastline and did not officially become a hurricane until two hours before it struck land.

At its strongest point, Hurricane Katrina blew 175-mile-per-hour (282 km/h) winds spanning more than 200 miles (322 km) across. The hurricane dropped up to 15 inches (38 cm) of rain. Katrina broke many of the levees protecting the city of New Orleans, flooding much of the city and destroying homes and roads. Levees are embankments built to protect an area against flooding from a nearby body of water. The levees in New Orleans were built to protect the city from the waters of the Gulf of Mexico, Lake Pontchartrain, and the Mississippi River.

atmosphere, and land. Without the water cycle there would be no rainfall and clouds would fail to form.

EARTH'S WATER CYCLE

Earth's water cycle does not start or stop in any one place. The water cycle's many steps are constantly changing the phase of water. This process keeps water moving around the globe. The role of each phase change in the water cycle is described in this chapter. Exactly

Figure 1.1   Flooding caused by Hurricane Katrina destroyed many areas in New Orleans, Louisiana.

Hurricane Katrina's destruction was devastating. The hurricane killed more than 2,000 people, left thousands of people homeless, and caused more than $80 billion in damages. It was the costliest hurricane in American history.[1, 2]

how each phase change occurs on a molecular level is described later in this book.

EVAPORATION

Evaporation is the process of changing a liquid into a gas and is an essential part of the planet's water cycle. Evaporation moves Earth's liquid water from the surface of the oceans, lakes, rivers, and streams into the atmosphere, where it resides temporarily as a gas.

The oceans, in particular, are a huge source of liquid water that is naturally evaporated in the planet's water cycle. About 70 percent of the surface of Earth is covered with oceans, so there is a large surface area where evaporation can take place.

On the surface of the oceans and other bodies of water, the Sun heats the liquid water molecules. This heat gives the molecules energy that allows them to break away from the forces holding them together as liquids to become a gas. In some cases, strong winds help speed up evaporation, physically assisting the liquid molecules in this process.

Over time, evaporation results in a large amount of water forming as a gas in the atmosphere. The gaseous form of water is called water vapor. Scientists estimate about 90 percent of water vapor in the atmosphere arrives there through the process of evaporation.[3]

CONDENSATION

Condensation is the reverse of evaporation. It is the process of changing a gas into a liquid. Much of the water vapor that enters the air due to evaporation at Earth's surface eventually condenses to form clouds. The amount and location of the water vapor can vary a lot, but there is always some water vapor in the air.

Condensation occurs above Earth's surface because of the unique pressure and temperature conditions. (**Pressure** is a measure of the number of times particles collide with the sides of a container.) Above Earth's surface, air is not confined to a container; but can be thought of as a giant mound of soil. The soil near the surface of Earth, at the bottom of the mound, is exposed to the weight of all the soil above it. The soil at the top of the mound isn't supporting much weight at all. So, air pressure at high altitudes is very low.

Although we can't see them, the layers of air in the atmosphere are similar to the mound of soil. Just like soil, air has weight. The air near the surface of Earth feels the pressure due to the weight of all the air above it. This makes near-surface air fairly condensed; that is, air particles are closer together. Air at the top of the pile (the top of the atmosphere) feels less pressure and less weight. Those particles are spread farther apart.

Second (and more influential), temperatures at high altitudes are very cold, because of the way the atmosphere is heated. Energy from the Sun warms Earth, which in turn warms the air above it. As a result, air nearer to Earth's surface is warmer than air higher and farther from the surface of the planet. This makes high-altitude air less condensed and very cold.

Low air pressure and low temperature are factors that affect the state of water. At certain altitudes, water is in a state of equilibrium between the gas state (water vapor) and the liquid state (liquid water). However, at higher altitudes colder temperatures will cause the water vapor to condense into liquid water or even change directly into crystals of ice. As water vapor particles condense, they combine with tiny particles of dust, salt, and smoke in the air to form water droplets. These water droplets can accumulate to form clouds.

Clouds are made up of condensed water droplets or ice crystals. Very high clouds are so cold that they are made of water droplets and ice. While most of the individual droplets are too small to fall as precipitation, collectively the many droplets are enough to make clouds visible from Earth. The water droplets within clouds tend to collide with each other. As they collide, the water droplets combine to form larger and larger water droplets. When the drops get big and heavy enough, they fall as precipitation.

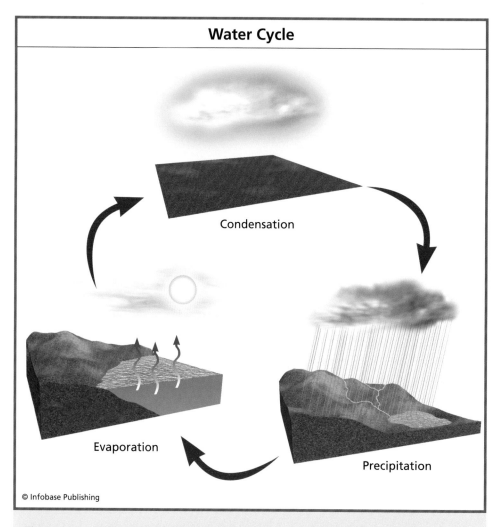

Water Cycle

Condensation

Evaporation

Precipitation

© Infobase Publishing

Figure 1.2   Water moves throughout Earth as a result of the water cycle. The three processes involved in the water cycle are evaporation, condensation, and precipitation.

MELTING

Melting is the process by which a solid changes into a liquid, and is the phase change that allows frozen water on Earth to be taken out of storage. In this case, a "stored" water particle is one that stays

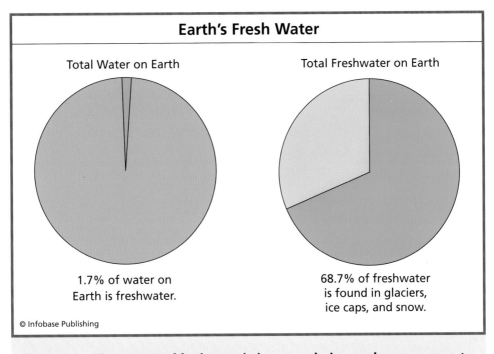

Earth's Fresh Water

Total Water on Earth

Total Freshwater on Earth

1.7% of water on
Earth is freshwater.

68.7% of freshwater
is found in glaciers,
ice caps, and snow.

© Infobase Publishing

Figure 1.3   The amount of freshwater in ice caps, glaciers, and snow represent a large percentage of Earth's total fresh water.

in the same place for a long time. It turns out there is much more water being stored on Earth in ice than there is in the rest of the water cycle at any given time. Being able to get all this water out of storage is an important part of the process.

Water is stored in a few ways. Lakes and oceans may store liquid water for weeks, months, or years. Underground aquifers can store liquid water for thousands of years. Glaciers, ice sheets, and ice caps can store frozen water for varying periods of time.

Seasonally, the melting of small glaciers and ice sheets on land provides fresh water for streams, rivers, and lakes. Over the winter, falling snow and precipitation build up in snowpacks in the mountains. When warm weather arrives in spring, both the snow and ice melt and feed local water systems. According to the U.S. Geological Survey, as much as 75 percent of the freshwater supply in the western United States comes from snowmelt.[4] Frozen water is also stored and melted seasonally for human use.

On much longer time scales, glaciers, ice sheets, and ice caps store fresh water for long-term use in the planet's water cycle. Melted water from these sources flows into the oceans and seeps

GLOBAL MELTING CONCERNS

Throughout Earth's history, the size of glaciers and ice sheets and the amount of melting has varied, but it has always been a key part of the water cycle. Today, scientists are concerned that our glaciers and ice sheets are melting fast—perhaps too fast.

According to the Worldwatch Institute, an independent research organization, melting of Earth's ice cover accelerated significantly in the 1990s. Worldwatch lists a number of changes in Earth's ice cover taken from many different research projects to support this claim. Evidence includes:

- Glaciers in Alaska are currently thinning twice as fast as they did from the 1950s to the mid-1990s.
- Glaciers in Montana are disappearing altogether (there were 150 in 1850; there are only 40 today).
- Glaciers in West Antarctica thinned much faster in 2002 and 2003 than in the 1990s.
- The edges of ice sheets in Greenland are melting ten times faster today than in 2001.[5]

Exactly why global ice seems to be melting quickly is a subject of much debate. Many people attribute warming global temperatures to human-induced causes. Others point to the planet's long record of changing ice cover and dismiss the melting as a normal part of Earth's history. But most agree, melting is happening faster now than it has in the past. What needs to be done, if anything, is another question.

into underground aquifers, where the water eventually comes out of storage and becomes part of the active water cycle.

Storage of water in glaciers and ice sheets is important because of sheer size. While glaciers, ice sheets, and ice caps do not hold the majority of Earth's water, they do hold the majority of the planet's fresh water (nearly 70 percent).[6] Without the simple phase change known as melting, we would not have access to these enormous reserves of fresh water.

FREEZING

Freezing, the opposite of melting, is the process by which a liquid changes into a solid. It is the phase change responsible for creating frozen forms of precipitation. Glaciers and ice sheets are formed as the result of the freezing process.

Freezing can happen in many different parts of Earth's atmosphere.

A snowflake is made up of ice crystals that are stuck together. Snowflakes form high in Earth's atmosphere. Hail is a frozen mass of water that often forms inside thunderstorms. Sleet is made up of drops of rain that freeze as they fall to Earth's surface. Freezing rain is precipitation that falls as liquid but freezes when it hits the cold ground. Together, these different forms of frozen precipitation move drops of liquid water out of the atmosphere and onto Earth's surface where they can melt and seep into oceans and groundwater or freeze and build up to create glaciers and ice sheets.

Glaciers are large, frozen rivers of snow and ice. Ice sheets are large areas of ice that usually cover land. Ice caps are large areas of ice, but are smaller than ice sheets. All three forms of ice require specific weather conditions to form and be maintained over time. Basically, a glacier begins when frozen precipitation falls and builds up in certain areas. In order for this build up to occur, summers must be cool enough not to melt the packed snow and ice every season. Usually, glaciers form at the North and South poles of the planet and at high mountain elevations. Every continent on Earth, including Africa, has at least one glacier.[7]

Over time, glaciers move and flow over the surface of Earth, carving distinct paths in the land. Glaciers melt, shrink, and grow over time, sometimes naturally and sometimes due to human climate changes brought about by human activities.

SUBLIMATION

Sublimation is the process by which a solid changes into a gas without going through the liquid phase. It is the phase change responsible for making snow disappear without melting.

Much of the time when snow disappears, it simply melts, making slush and puddles of liquid water. But under certain conditions, snow undergoes sublimation and changes directly from solid snow back into water vapor.

Snow sublimation happens particularly often in the western United States, where warm, dry winds often blow after an intense cold spell. When these warm, dry winds blow over an area covered in snow, the snow sublimates directly to a gas, skipping the liquid phase entirely. In some areas, this wind is known as the "Chinook Wind;" (*Chinook* is a Native American word that means "snow eater."[8]) Although sublimation plays a less vital role in the planet's water cycle than some other phase changes, such as evaporation and condensation, it still serves to move water around Earth.

DEPOSITION

Deposition is the process by which a gas changes into a solid without going through the liquid phase. It is the opposite of sublimation. Deposition is responsible for creating snow at high altitudes and the formation of frost on cold winter days.

While some snow is formed high in the atmosphere from freezing water droplets, most snow actually forms via deposition. Water vapor in the air turns directly into solid snow, skipping the liquid phase altogether.

Deposition also occurs when frost forms on chilly winter mornings. The water vapor in the air comes in contact with a super-cold surface, such as the windshield of a car, and freezes immediately into tiny ice crystals. Because of the cold temperatures a liquid never forms, and the water vapor changes directly into a solid.

Like sublimation, deposition plays a lesser role in the water cycle than some other phase changes, but it is no less important to the overall process. Deposition moves gaseous water in the air into the planet's water cycle.

You've likely seen or heard about many of the phase changes that happen regularly as part of Earth's water cycle. But why do they happen? How do they happen? Ultimately, the answers lie in how molecules behave inside matter. This behavior determines if a substance takes the solid, liquid, or gaseous form, and when it changes from one state to another.

The Behavior
of Molecules

Think about the different levels of activity in the rooms at your school. Some rooms are quiet, such as crowded classrooms where students are taking tests. No one moves much and everyone is seated in the room in some orderly fashion. Other rooms are loud and there is constant motion, such as the cafeteria at lunchtime. Everyone moves from place to place in no particular pattern.

Each room in your school has its own set of predictable rules and behaviors, its own "state of chaos." How students move, behave, and occupy a space determines the state of chaos. Once you learn the state of chaos for a given room at school (the test-taking room, for example), you can predict what the students will do in that room, or state.

In the same way, the behavior of molecules in chemistry determines the **state of matter**, or phase of a substance. The state of matter tells you how molecules move, behave, and are organized in space. Like the students in the school, once you learn the state of matter for a given object, you can predict what the molecules will do in that state. To understand how molecules behave to determine an object's state of matter, it helps to learn some basic chemistry vocabulary first.

IMPORTANT TERMS

Before one can understand a state of matter, it's good to understand the basic definitions of **matter** and all of its parts. Matter, it turns out, includes everything on Earth. That is, anything that has mass and takes up space. Trees, books, and computers are all types of matter. So are air, steam, and stars. Matter comes in countless shapes and forms, and is made up of many different substances called **elements**.

Elements are the most basic substances in the universe. They can only be broken down into their most basic components by scientists in a laboratory. Elements, however, do not usually break down naturally. Oxygen, carbon, and copper are all examples of elements. So are calcium, titanium, and seaborgium. Everything on Earth is made of elements.

The elements have been organized in a chart called the **periodic table**—one of the most useful tools in all of chemistry. The periodic table is an organized chart that provides information about individual and groups of elements. There are currently 111 elements known. Instead of memorizing the properties for every element, chemists simply consult the periodic table. One thing the periodic table can tell you about is the structure of each element.

An **atom** is the smallest part of an element that still maintains the properties of that element. An atom is the fundamental unit of an element. Atoms of different elements vary in size, but all of them are too small to be seen with the human eye. An optical microscope, even a powerful one, can't show an atom. In general, if you could line up two hundred million atoms side by side, they would make a line about one centimeter long. Scientists use special

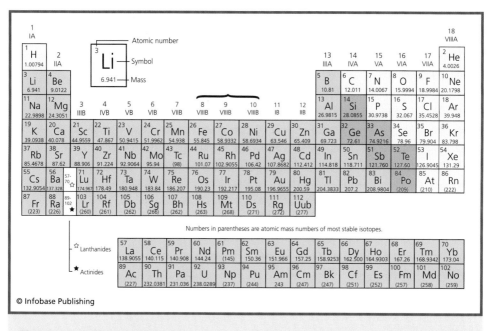

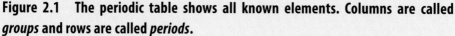

© Infobase Publishing

Figure 2.1 The periodic table shows all known elements. Columns are called *groups* and rows are called *periods*.

microscopes, such as a scanning tunneling microscope or the atomic force microscope, to produce images of atoms.

Atoms of different elements combine in different ways to create new substances. Water, for example, is made when atoms of hydrogen and oxygen bond together in a particular way. Salt is made when atoms of the elements sodium and chlorine bond together.

Some combinations of different atoms are called **molecules**. Technically, a molecule is made when two or more atoms bond together. Most things on Earth are made of these multi-element molecules.

Chemists express atoms and molecules as letters or series of letters. Each element usually has a one- or two-letter chemical symbol. The letter "H," for example, stands for the element hydrogen. "Na" stands for the element sodium.

Scientists use **chemical formulas** as a short way to show the elements that make up a molecule of a substance. A chemical formula includes the symbols of each element that makes up the molecule. The formula for water, for example, is "H_2O." This chemical formula shows that two hydrogen atoms are bonded to one oxygen atom in one molecule of water.

INSIDE THE ATOM

The forces that bond atoms together to form molecules come from tiny, **subatomic particles** called **protons** and **electrons**. These particles have different electrical charges that attract each other.

At the center of the atom is the **nucleus**, a densely packed area of positively charged protons and neutral **neutrons**. The positively charged nucleus attracts negatively charged particles called **electrons**. The electrons can be found in an area that surrounds the nucleus called the electron cloud. Inside the electron cloud are shells and orbitals where electrons are most likely to be found. It is these clouds of moving electrons that allow the atom to form bonds with other atoms.

CHEMICAL BONDS

A **chemical bond** forms when atoms gain, lose, or share electrons. How electrons from two or more atoms interact determines the type of chemical bond formed. The interaction of electrons depends on the location and number of electrons in the atom.

ELECTRON LOCATION

The location of electrons in an atom is one factor that determines how that atom will form bonds with other atoms. Scientists use two basic models to explain the location of electrons in the atom—the Bohr model and the quantum mechanics model.

The Bohr model was developed in 1913 and describes electrons orbiting the nucleus being held in place with energy. In the

TABLE 2.1 VOCABULARY AT A GLANCE

WORD	DEFINITION	EXAMPLES
Matter	Anything that has mass and takes up space.	Humans, telephones, oranges, air
Element	The most basic substances in the universe.	Carbon (C), iron (Fe), hydrogen (H)
Atom	The smallest piece of an element that maintains the properties of that element.	Helium atom

Bohr model, the energy levels are called **orbits**. The way electrons move along fixed orbits around the nucleus of an atom is similar to the way the planets orbit the Sun. This is the original, somewhat primitive model for the atom. The Bohr model works well for very simple atoms, but is no longer used in more complex chemistry.

The quantum mechanics model is more modern and more mathematical. It describes a volume of space surrounding the nucleus of an atom where electrons reside, referred to earlier as the electron cloud. Similar to the Bohr model, the quantum mechanics model shows that electrons can be found in energy levels. Electrons do not, however, follow fixed paths around the nucleus. According to the quantum mechanics model, the exact location of an electron cannot be known, but there are areas in the electron cloud where there is a high probability that electrons can be found. These areas are the energy levels; each energy level contains sublevels. The areas in which electrons are located in sublevels are called atomic **orbitals**. The exact location of the electrons in the clouds cannot be precisely predicted, but the unique speed, direction, spin, orientation, and distance from the nucleus of each electron in an atom can be considered. The quantum mechanics model is much more complicated, and accurate, than the Bohr model.

WORD	DEFINITION	EXAMPLES
Subatomic particles	Tiny particles inside an atom.	Neutrons, electrons, and protons
Molecule	Two or more atoms bonded together.	Water molecule
Chemical bond	Created when atoms give, take, or share electrons.	H:H Formula used to show the bonding between 2 hydrogen atoms
Chemical formula	Describes atoms or molecules using the letter symbols of each element.	H_2O The chemical formula for water

ELECTRON NUMBER

The number of electrons in an atom is a second factor that determines how that atom will form bonds. Atoms whose outermost energy level contains the maximum number of electrons allowed are the most stable. A stable atom is one that does not easily gain, lose, or share electrons.

As stated earlier, electrons can be found in orbitals within the energy levels of an atom. Each energy level has a different number of orbitals. For example, energy level 1 of all atoms has one orbital. This orbital can hold two electrons. Therefore, energy level 1 can hold only two electrons. Energy level 2 has four orbitals. That means that energy level 2 can hold eight electrons.

The orbitals in an energy level are considered a shell. An atom becomes stable when the shell in its outermost energy level contains the maximum number of electrons that level can hold. For most common elements that means eight electrons in the shell of the outermost energy level. Energy levels farther from the nucleus hold multiple orbitals. Therefore, the farther an energy level is from the nucleus, the more energy it contains.

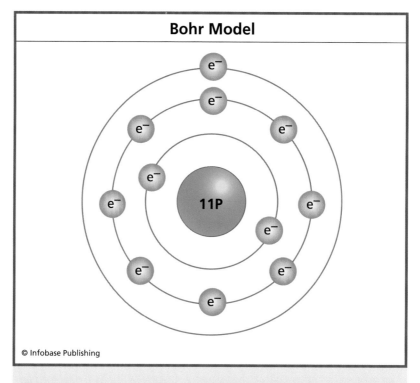

Bohr Model

11P

© Infobase Publishing

Figure 2.2   The Bohr atom was proposed by Niels Bohr. He believed that electrons moved around the nucleus similar to the way planets orbit the Sun.

Electrons fill the orbitals in the lowest energy level first, and then proceed to fill up the orbitals in other energy levels. If an atom has only two electrons, such as the element helium, those two electrons fill the lowest energy level, and the atom is stable. A helium atom does not easily gain, lose, or share electrons because its only orbital is full.

Atoms with eight electrons in their outermost energy level are also considered stable. The tendency to become stable with eight electrons in the outermost energy level is called the **octet rule**. The octet rule is the driving force behind bond formation, because atoms will react with each other until each atom becomes stable.

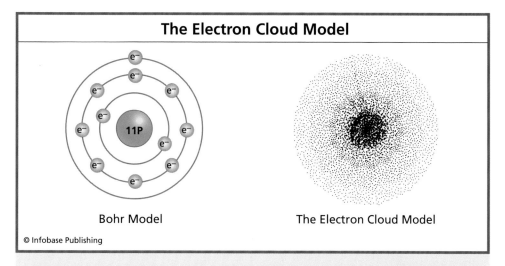

The Electron Cloud Model

Bohr Model

The Electron Cloud Model

© Infobase Publishing

Figure 2.3   The quantum mechanics model proposes that the location of electrons cannot be precisely known, but there are areas where electrons are likely to be found.

Atoms that are stable are labeled *unreactive*. Atoms that readily gain, lose, or share electrons to fill their energy levels are labeled *reactive*. Atoms with one electron in its outer level will easily lose or share their electrons. Atoms with six or seven electrons in that level readily gain electrons to become stable.

When atoms gain, lose, or share electrons with other atoms they create chemical bonds. It is these chemical bonds that hold atoms together to form molecules.

TABLE 2.2 ENERGY LEVELS, ORBITALS, AND ELECTRONS IN ATOMS		
ENERGY LEVEL	NUMBER OF ORBITALS	NUMBER OF ELECTRONS
1	1	2
2	4	8
3	9	18
4	16	32

THE BEHAVIOR OF MOLECULES IN GROUPS

Chemical bonds are the strongest forces acting between atoms in a molecule. The force attracting hydrogen atoms to oxygen atoms in a water molecule, for example, is very strong. The forces acting between whole molecules are much weaker. The force attracting one water molecule to another water molecule in a cup of water, for example, is not as strong as the chemical bond between the atoms within each water molecule. On the other hand, these weak whole-molecule forces determine how groups of molecules relate to one another and, in turn, determine the state of matter of that substance.

Chemists recognize three main states of matter: solid, liquid, and gas. The molecules inside each state of matter move and behave in specific ways, depending on the forces involved. These behaviors determine the two main characteristics that determine an object's state of matter: shape and volume.

An object has **shape** when its dimensions can be measured. A solid piece of ice, for example, may be measured as a cube measuring 1 inch by 1 inch by 1 inch. It has a defined, measurable shape that is hard to change. A liquid and a gas, by contrast, have no dimensions and no sides that can be measured without a container. If you have liquid water, it takes the shape of whatever container it is in. The same principle applies when you fill a balloon with air. The air fills the shape of the balloon. If you spill a glass of water, the liquid will spread out on a surface and not retain its shape. A solid has a defined shape, but liquids and gases do not.

An object has **volume** when it occupies a defined amount of space. A glass of water, for example, can be measured as 16 ounces. It has a defined, measurable volume. Solids have defined, measurable volumes as well. But a gas can disperse in the air and spread out. The gas molecules are still present, but they are not contained in a defined amount of space. Gases that are not in closed containers do not have defined volumes.

TABLE 2.3 PROPERTIES OF EACH STATE OF MATTER		
STATE OF MATTER	SHAPE	VOLUME
Solid	Yes	Yes
Liquid	No	Yes
Gas	No	No

Shape and volume help determine the state of a sample of matter. They also tell you a lot about how the atoms and molecules are behaving inside that sample. It is the behavior of the atoms in an object that ultimately determines that object's properties.

A **property** is a characteristic behavior of a chemical substance. For example, most metals at room temperature are hard, shiny solids that retain their shape and volume. These are commonly recognized properties of metals. A liquid easily spreads when it is spilled. This is a commonly recognized property of liquids.

CHANGING BEHAVIORS

One of the most interesting things about an object's state of matter is that it can change. The behavior and organization of atoms and molecules in states of matter are not permanent. A solid can become a liquid; a liquid can become a gas; a gas can become a solid. Any change from one state of matter to another is physically possible under the right conditions.

State-of-matter changes, or phase changes, usually depend on the surrounding temperature and pressure. Evaporation, condensation, sublimation, and deposition are examples of common phase changes that often happen naturally on Earth. Chemists can also produce phase changes by manipulating temperatures and pressures in controlled environments.

Water is a common example of a substance that changes state fairly easily with changing temperature. At room temperature, water is a liquid. Drop the temperature to freezing (32°F/ 0°C), and water becomes solid ice. Raise the temperature to boiling (212°F/100°C), and water becomes a gas. Simply by changing the temperature of water, you can cause its state to change.

Solids, Liquids, and Gases

Solids, liquids, and gases are classified as different states of matter because each has a different way of organizing its atoms and molecules. Molecules in a solid are tightly packed, while molecules in a gas move freely.

This organization of molecules is important because it gives each state of matter its own set of unique properties. Tightly-packed solids are often hard, while gases, with their freely moving molecules, have no defined shape. This chapter examines the organization of atoms and molecules in solids, liquids, and gases, plus some of the resulting properties.

SOLIDS

Particles in a solid are organized, tightly packed together, and don't move around or mix together. Because of their fixed positions, solids have their own shape. The size of the atoms or molecules that make up a substance are one thing that determines how they are organized in a solid. Atoms of different elements vary in size; some are smaller or larger than others. When atoms of different sizes are packed tightly together, unique structures result.

The atoms in a molecule of table salt (NaCl), for example, are of different sizes. The sodium (Na) atoms are smaller than the larger chlorine (Cl) atoms, so the sodium atoms become packed in between the larger chlorine atoms. The resulting shape is a crystal, building-block structure. The atoms are as tightly packed as possible, but there is still a lot of space inside the crystal structure because of the difference in size of the atoms involved.

Solids made up of only one element, by contrast, have atoms of equal size. All hydrogen atoms, for example, are the same size. This results in what chemists call a **close-packed structure**, where each atom is located as close to the next atom as possible. Not much space is wasted because the equal-sized atoms fit snugly together. The atoms in metals, for example, are often arranged in close-packed structures.

The forces acting between molecules or atoms in a solid substance are the second factor that determines how atoms or molecules are organized within the solid. Forces can be strong, such as chemical bonds between atoms (think of these as having superglue strength); or they can be weak, such as **intermolecular forces** (think of these as having weaker, rubber cement strength). Basically, an intermolecular force is nothing more than a force of attraction between two or more molecules.

Amorphous Solids and Crystalline Solids

There are two types of solids: amorphous solids and crystalline solids.

The molecules in **amorphous** solids are held together by unpredictable bonds and forces. The molecules are also arranged in a random manner. Amorphous solids have no definite geometric

Figure 3.1 The mineral beryl has a definite geometric pattern that makes it a crystalline solid.

pattern. Examples of amorphous solids include glass, rubber, and plastic.

In these solids, there can be many different types of molecules bonding in many different ways. Some molecules may be held in place by chemical bonds, others by intermolecular forces. Because of the different forces in action, these solids are often not quite as organized and predictable as some others. As a result, amorphous solids exhibit a range of different properties.

Glass, for example, is an amorphous solid that is hard, brittle, and difficult to melt. Rubber and plastic, by contrast, are amorphous solids that are soft and easy to melt. Because there are many different forces holding atoms together in amorphous solids, there are many different properties as well.

Most solids are **crystalline solids**. The atoms and molecules in crystalline solids are arranged in definite geometric patterns. Each geometric pattern piece is called a unit cell. Unit cells repeat over and over in the solid. Think of each unit cell as a building block. Within each crystalline solid, the exact organization of the atoms and molecules depends on two things: size and force. Depending on the types of forces holding atoms or molecules together in a solid, chemists group crystalline solids into four main categories: ionic solids, metallic solids, network atomic solids, and molecular solids.

Ionic Solids

The atoms in an **ionic solid** are held together by forces between charged particles. Charged particles are called ions. The forces create a type of chemical bond known as an **ionic bond**.

An ionic bond forms when one atom gives an electron to another atom. In its natural state, an atom is neutral. When an ionic bond is formed between atoms, however, the atoms become charged particles, that is, they become ions.

The atom that gives away one or more electrons loses its negative charge and becomes positively charged. Chemists call this positively charged atom a **cation**. The atom that takes one or more electrons receives extra negative charge. Chemists call this negatively charged atom an **anion**. This give and take of electrons results in an ionic bond between two oppositely charged atoms, creating an ionic molecule.

Each ionic molecule has a cation end and an anion end. The oppositely charged ends of different molecules are naturally attracted to each other because opposites attract. This force can hold ionically bonded molecules together in an ionic solid.

A common example of an ionic solid is table salt (NaCl). Table salt is created when one atom of sodium (Na) creates an ionic bond with one atom of chlorine (Cl). Sodium loses its one outer electron (becoming a cation, Na^+) while chlorine takes this electron (becoming an anion, Cl^-). The Na^+ cation bonds with the Cl^- anion to form NaCl, common table salt.

Even though the atoms are bonded together, they still maintain the positive and negative charges on each end. It would be very rare to have just one particle of sodium chloride. When two NaCl

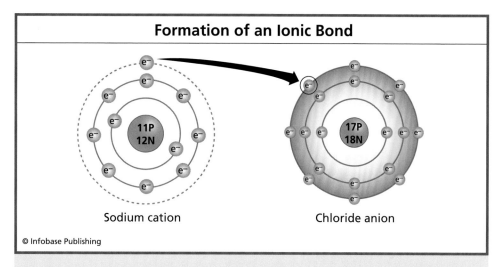

Formation of an Ionic Bond

Sodium cation

Chloride anion

© Infobase Publishing

Figure 3.2 In an ionic bond between sodium and chlorine, the sodium atom loses its outermost electron to the chlorine atom. The sodium becomes positively charged (cation) and the chlorine becomes negatively charged (anion).

particles come together, the Na^+ atom of one particle is attracted to the Cl^- atom of another particle. This type of attraction continues as billions and billions and billions of NaCl particles stick together very closely to form a crystal. This force between molecules, called an **electrostatic force**, holds the atoms tightly in place in the ionic solid.

As a result of the strong forces holding atoms together in an ionic solid, certain properties result. Ionic solids typically have very high melting and boiling points, for example, because it takes a lot of energy to break the atoms in the solid apart. A lot of energy (in terms of heat) must be added to break the forces holding atoms together and cause them to melt or boil.

Metallic Solids

The atoms in a **metallic solid** are held together by forces created when many atoms share electrons. These forces create a type of chemical bond known as a **metallic bond**.

A metallic bond occurs when a pool of electrons forms a bond with the atoms of a metal. The atoms that make up a piece of metal are cations rather than neutral atoms. The valence electrons of metals surround the cations. Valence electrons in a metal are freely floating particles, sometimes called a *sea of electrons*, that move around the cations. The valence electrons are attracted to the cations, forming metallic bonds. Metallic bonds hold particles of metals together.

Picture a piece of silver (Ag). The Ag cations are surrounded by valence electrons. The metallic bond, which is the attraction between the positive cations and the negative valence electrons, holds that piece of silver together.

The resulting force between atoms is strong and holds atoms tightly in place. This strength determines many of the properties we commonly associate with metals. Most metals are malleable because of the tightly packed atoms, and they are often not easy to melt because separating the atoms requires a lot of heat energy.

Another common property of metals is that they are good conductors of electricity. This results from the pool of free-floating, constantly moving valence electrons. These electrons can carry an electric current through the piece of metal. After all, an electric current is nothing more than the moving of charged electrons. Most electrical wires are made of metal to take advantage of this important property.

Network Atomic Solids

The atoms in network atomic solids are held together by forces created when electrons are shared between atoms. These forces create a type of chemical bond known as a covalent bond.

A **covalent bond** occurs when two atoms, both in need of electrons to become stable, share electrons. Instead of one atom giving an electron to another atom, the atoms overlap and share one or more electrons that are still bound to their nuclei.

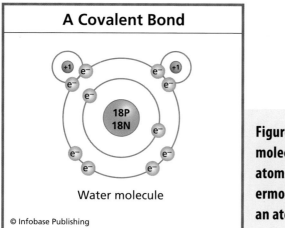

A Covalent Bond

18P
18N

Water molecule

© Infobase Publishing

Figure 3.3   In a water molecule, two hydrogen atoms share their outermost electrons with an atom of oxygen.

A covalent bond commonly found in nature is two hydrogen atoms bonded together (H_2). Hydrogen has only a single electron, but it only needs two electrons in its one electron shell to become stable. In this case, a hydrogen atom won't give its only electron away. Instead, it often shares its electron with another hydrogen atom, forming H_2.

Individual H_2 and other covalent molecules are often quite small, occurring between only a handful of atoms. One molecule of water, for example, is composed of two hydrogen atoms covalently bound to a single oxygen atom. This makes one tiny, stable molecule. None of these three atoms will form additional covalent bonds with other atoms.

Sometimes atoms or molecules can form covalent bonds with many other atoms or molecules to make huge structures that can be seen. These are called *network atomic solids* and can form when a covalent bond occurs between many atoms or molecules at the same time.

Like a metallic solid, groups of atoms share electrons in a network atomic solid. But in this case, each electron is still tightly bound to its own, original nucleus. This creates a very strong force holding multiple atoms together. One known property of network atomic solids is that they are some of the hardest substances found on the planet.

The hardest network atomic solid—in fact, the hardest (currently) known material on the planet—is a type of carbon that forms diamonds. The covalently bonded arrangement of carbon atoms within diamonds forms naturally at intense temperatures and pressures inside the Earth.

Most diamonds are formed about 90 miles (145 km) underground, where extreme heat and strong pressure allow carbon crystal structures to grow large. Over time (some say as long as 50 million years), these diamond structures make their way to the surface of Earth and are mined from the rock by humans. About 25 countries operate active diamond mines today, and diamonds are known to exist on every continent except Europe and Antarctica.

Molecular Solids

The atoms in **molecular solids** are held together by weak intermolecular forces. These forces are much weaker than the chemical bonds in ionic, metallic, and network atomic solids, but they are still strong enough to hold molecules together.

Frozen water is a good example of a solid that is held together by intermolecular forces. Each water molecule has two hydrogen atoms that are covalently bonded to one oxygen atom (H_2O). The hydrogen atoms share their electrons with the oxygen atom. As a result of the unique molecular shape that forms, the hydrogen end of the molecule has a positive charge and the oxygen end has a negative charge.

The positively charged ends of hydrogen atoms are attracted to the negatively charged ends of nearby oxygen atoms in other water molecules. These intermolecular forces are weaker than the chemical bonds seen in ionic solids, but strong enough to hold the molecules together when water freezes to become a solid.

These relatively weak bonds help determine the properties of ice. The molecules are held together by weak forces: as a result, they are easy to break apart. It requires little energy, in this case heat, to overcome the forces and separate the molecules in ice to make liquid water.

LIQUIDS

Atoms in a liquid are packed together in a defined space in a semi-organized way, but those atoms are able to move around freely and sometimes mix in unpredictable ways. Unlike solids, there is no set organization or strong bonding between atoms in a liquid. But like a solid, the forces between atoms are what make a liquid a liquid, giving this state of matter its own unique properties. Liquids can mix, spill, and change shape easily.

Because the molecules in a liquid move freely, a simple stir with a spoon causes the molecules to mix and rearrange. But mixing doesn't rearrange the molecules to create a new substance. Mixing doesn't destroy the molecular arrangement of the liquid. The liquid remains a liquid.

Sometimes two different liquids will not mix together, such as oil and water. The intermolecular forces within each individual liquid are stronger than the force of mixing. Each liquid can be mixed individually, but the two will not stay mixed together.

The forces that keep the liquid together when mixed are the same forces that keep a spilled liquid together. When you pour a glass of water on the floor, it will form a puddle. The molecules will not spread out infinitely in every direction (as they would in a gas) because the molecules are held together just tight enough to maintain the original liquid.

The forces that hold liquids together are also responsible for the third unique property of liquids: the ability to change shape. Imagine a balloon filled with water. You can push or pull the balloon to change the shape of the water without ever changing the molecular structure of the water or the amount of the water inside. The water always assumes the shape of the balloon.

The intermolecular forces that hold molecules together in a liquid tend to be weaker than actual chemical bonds. These forces allow molecules to stick together but still be able to mix and move. There are three types of intermolecular forces that hold atoms together in liquids: hydrogen bonds, dipole-dipole forces, and dispersion forces.

DIPOLE-DIPOLE INTERACTION

Dipole-dipole interactions are a type of intermolecular force that occurs when the positively charged end of one molecule is attracted to the negatively charged end of another molecule. In this case, a **dipole** is nothing more than a molecule with a charge.

Hydrochloric acid is an example of a molecule that exhibits dipole-dipole forces between molecules. Hydrochloric acid is made of one hydrogen atom (H^+) and one chlorine (Cl^-) atom. The chemical formula for hydrochloric acid is HCl. In this case, the hydrogen atom gives its electron to the chlorine atom to form a chemical bond.

The dipole-dipole interaction occurs when the chlorine atom in one molecule is attracted to the hydrogen atom in another molecule. This attraction occurs because the chlorine atom in an HCl molecule is negatively charged (it has an extra electron) and the hydrogen atom in an HCl molecule is positively charged (it gave away its only electron). Graphically, they look something like this:

$$H^+Cl^- \text{ --- } H^+Cl^-$$

The dipole-dipole forces that join such molecules together are much weaker than both the chemical bonds joining the atoms within the molecule and the hydrogen bonds formed in other situations. But it is still a powerful enough force to affect the behavior of a group of molecules.

Hydrogen Bond

Hydrogen bonds are a type of intermolecular force that occurs when a hydrogen atom (H^+) is attracted to an atom in another

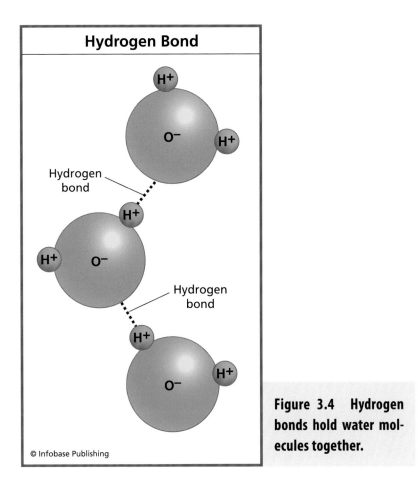

Hydrogen Bond

Hydrogen bond

Hydrogen bond

© Infobase Publishing

Figure 3.4 Hydrogen bonds hold water molecules together.

molecule. This particular bond strongly affects how groups of molecules behave.

Hydrogen always occurs in nature as H_2 because a single atom (H^+) has only one electron. To fill its energy level and become stable, the single hydrogen atom shares its electron with another hydrogen atom to form H_2. It is the H_2 molecule that is involved in hydrogen bonding.

The hydrogen molecule (H_2) is particularly attractive to a few elements, including fluorine (F), chlorine (Cl), bromine (Br), and iodine (I). These four elements are each highly **electronegative**, meaning they readily attract electrons to form a stable octet.

Water is a good example of hydrogen bonding. A hydrogen bond is formed between water molecules when a hydrogen atom in one water molecule is attracted to an oxygen atom in another water molecule. The hydrogen bonds that join molecules together are much weaker than the chemical bonds that join atoms together. Graphically, hydrogen bonds look something like this:

Such hydrogen bonds create an intermolecular force that joins multiple water molecules together in a group and affects their behavior. Hydrogen bonds are actually just extremely strong dipole-dipole interactions. This is why it takes a lot of energy to boil water compared to other liquids that do not contain hydrogen bonds.

Dispersion Force

Dispersion forces are a type of intermolecular force that occurs when molecules become temporarily charged, either positively or negatively, and become attracted to each other.

This force involves molecules that are usually neutral. But in all molecules, electrons are constantly moving around the atomic nuclei. As a result, there are brief times when all the electrons gather in one location and charge one end of the atom or molecule. When the charged end appears, it can temporarily attract other molecules with an opposite charge.

The dispersion forces between chlorine molecules (Cl_2) are one example. Chlorine molecules are formed when one chlorine atom shares its one electron with another chlorine atom to form a chemical bond. The "shared" electrons are actually moving back and forth between atoms in constant movement, temporarily creating a charge on one end of the Cl_2 molecule. Graphically, it looks some-thing like this:

$$Cl^+\text{-}Cl^- \text{ --- } Cl^+\text{-}Cl^-$$

This type of intermolecular force is very weak and short lived, but it can still affect the behavior of a group of molecules.

GASES

Particles in a gas are far apart, fast-moving, and are not organized in any particular way. Unlike the particles in solids and liquids, the atoms and molecules in gases are not particularly attracted to each other.

In gases, the intermolecular forces that hold molecules together in liquids and some solids are still present, but gas molecules over-come these intermolecular forces with speed. Individual gas mol-ecules are always on the move; they have a lot of energy that keeps them moving constantly.

As a result, within a gas, the atoms or molecules pass each other regularly and interact only for a brief moment of time. This short bit of time is not enough for intermolecular forces to take hold and act. As a result, the atoms and molecules in a gas continue on their own way.

This lack of force holding atoms or molecules together is what determines the most unique properties of gases.

A gas will expand in all directions to fill any space, and will spread to take on the shape of its container. But it is not the same as a liquid. You can fill a glass with water and the water will spread to take the shape of the glass, and will mix and move when prompted. But the water will not spontaneously leave the glass.

By contrast, you cannot fill an open glass with gas and expect the gas to stay there. The gas will disperse out of the glass and fill the room. Gas flows and changes shape like a liquid, but more so.

Figure 3.5 Heated gases fill a hot-air balloon causing the balloon to expand and rise.

There are no other forces, with the exception of gravity, to hold a gas in place.

In this state of matter, it's not so much the forces acting between atoms or molecules that are important. Instead, three other factors determine the movements of atoms or molecules in a gas: temperature, pressure, and volume. Chemists relate these three factors in a series of gas laws. These factors and the gas laws are discussed in the following pages.

Temperature

Temperature is not just about how hot or cold something feels. **Temperature** is actually a measurement of the average **kinetic energy** in a material. Kinetic energy refers to the energy of motion. Particles within matter are always in motion. The faster the particles within a sample of matter move, the higher its kinetic energy, or temperature.

The slower the particles move, the lower its kinetic energy, or temperature. Gases at warm temperatures have fast-moving particles.

Pressure

Pressure is a measure of force exerted on a surface. In a gas, pressure is the amount of force exerted by atoms or molecules when they collide with the sides of a container. The atoms or molecules in a gas move in random directions, but they eventually hit something. The air in a tire, for example, is constantly moving. When the air hits the walls of the tire, the impact is measured as pressure. All gases exert some amount of pressure.

Volume

Volume is simply a defined amount of space. The air inside a tire, for example, occupies a defined space, so it has a defined volume. Volume is important to gases, because if a space is not defined, gases will disperse in every direction. Unlike a liquid that will puddle or a solid that sticks firmly together, a gas will spread infinitely in space. To hold or study a gas, a container with a defined space or volume is needed.

The Ideal Gas Law

Temperature, pressure, and volume interact to determine how a gas behaves. Chemists have defined the relationship between these three factors in a series of gas laws—rules about how gases behave. Because it is difficult to observe and study the tiny atoms or molecules in a constantly moving gas, the gas laws are used to predict and explain the behavior of atoms or molecules in a gas.

Throughout history there have been multiple versions of gas laws developed and named after many different people. Boyle's Law (1662), Charles's Law (1802), and Avogadro's Law (1811) are a few examples.

Today, most of those laws have been combined into what chemists call the **ideal gas law**. The ideal gas law is written as an equation using letters in place of numbers. Each letter stands for a different factor that can be measured for a specific gas. The equation for the ideal gas law is:

$$PV = nRT$$

P stands for pressure, V stands for volume, n is the number of gas particles, R is a constant (a predetermined, known number), and T stands for temperature.

Chemists use the equation to determine the pressure, volume, amount, or temperature for a specific gas. For example, say you know the volume and temperature of the air in a car tire. To

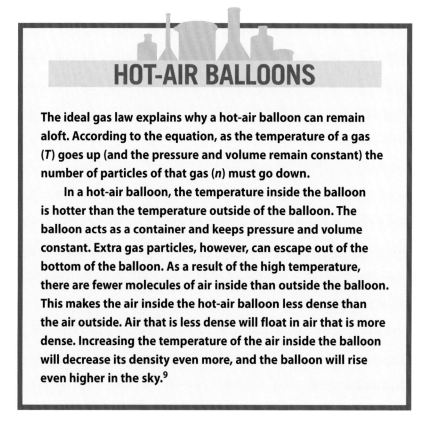

HOT-AIR BALLOONS

The ideal gas law explains why a hot-air balloon can remain aloft. According to the equation, as the temperature of a gas (T) goes up (and the pressure and volume remain constant) the number of particles of that gas (n) must go down.

In a hot-air balloon, the temperature inside the balloon is hotter than the temperature outside of the balloon. The balloon acts as a container and keeps pressure and volume constant. Extra gas particles, however, can escape out of the bottom of the balloon. As a result of the high temperature, there are fewer molecules of air inside than outside the balloon. This makes the air inside the hot-air balloon less dense than the air outside. Air that is less dense will float in air that is more dense. Increasing the temperature of the air inside the balloon will decrease its density even more, and the balloon will rise even higher in the sky.[9]

calculate the pressure being exerted on the inside of the tire, you would plug the known numbers into the equation and solve for *P*.

The drawback to this equation is that the "ideal gas law" gets its name because it only works for "ideal" or perfect gases. Unfortunately, ideal gases do not really exist. No gas will fit this equation perfectly, but some fit better than others. Regardless, the ideal gas law is commonly used to estimate and understand how the atoms and molecules in a gas behave.

Evaporation and Condensation

Evaporation occurs when a liquid changes to a gas. Condensation is the opposite of evaporation; it occurs when a gas changes to a liquid.

You can see rapid evaporation in action any time you boil a pot of water. When you boil water, you are using thermal energy, or heat, to change water from a liquid to a gas. You know evaporation is working when the gaseous water, or steam, makes the teapot whistle.

You see condensation every time you leave a cold beverage in the sun. In a very short time, drops of water begin to form on the outside of the glass. These droplets form when air touching the cold glass is cooled. Water vapor in the air around the glass condenses to form liquid droplets on the sides of the glass.

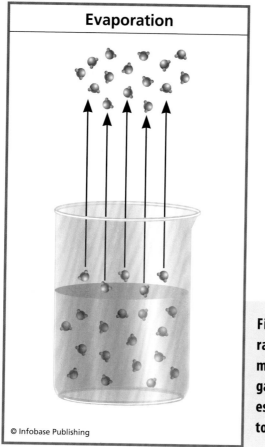

Evaporation

© Infobase Publishing

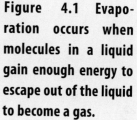

Figure 4.1 Evaporation occurs when molecules in a liquid gain enough energy to escape out of the liquid to become a gas.

Evaporation and condensation depend entirely on how much energy each particle in a substance contains. In the above examples, when the water molecules got enough energy to overcome the intermolecular forces holding them together, they evaporated to become a gas, water vapor. Likewise, when the water vapor molecules cooled, they lost energy and slowed down, eventually condensing to form a liquid.

This chapter takes a closer look at the energy particles in a liquid, the forces they exert, and how they change during evaporation and condensation.

THE ENERGY OF MOLECULES IN A LIQUID

All the particles—atoms and molecules—in a liquid have a certain amount of energy. This energy allows them to move and flow throughout the liquid, frequently bumping into each other in the process.

When one molecule bumps into another molecule, energy is transferred between those molecules. One molecule departs the collision with a little more energy than it started with, while the other molecule departs with a little less energy. As a result, all the molecules in a liquid have energy—but not all have the exact same amount of energy.

The temperature of a material is a measure of the average kinetic energy of all the molecules measured that make up the material. When the temperature of a liquid rises, the change indicates that the molecules in that liquid are gaining more and more energy and moving faster. The faster the molecules move, the higher the temperature.

Eventually, the kinetic energy of each molecule is great enough to overcome the intermolecular forces holding those molecules together in the liquid state. When this happens, the high-energy molecules evaporate and the state of matter changes from a liquid to a gas (Figure 4.1).

The opposite occurs when energy is removed from a gas. The molecules in the gas slow down and the temperature falls. The slower the molecules move, the lower the temperature. Eventually, the kinetic energy of each molecule is too slow and the molecules give in to intermolecular forces that eventually bind the molecules together as a liquid. When this happens, the low-energy gas molecules condense into a liquid.

THE FORCES IN A LIQUID

Most liquids are held together by intermolecular forces. But not all intermolecular forces are equal. The strength of the intermolecular force holding a material in the liquid state determines how much energy (usually heat) needs to be added to a liquid to change it to a gas, and how much energy needs to be taken away from a gas to change it to a liquid.

To understand the importance of the intermolecular forces in these phase changes, compare two common liquids: water and acetone, a common ingredient in nail polish remover. The hydrogen bonds that hold molecules together in water are much stronger than the dipole-dipole forces that hold molecules together in acetone. Because the intermolecular forces holding acetone molecules together are weak, it takes very little energy for liquid acetone to evaporate. As a result, acetone boils at a low temperature and has a very strong smell, two properties not commonly associated with water.

In order to provide enough energy for water molecules to evaporate, heat must be added. Water must be heated to a temperature of 212°F (100°C) in order for individual water molecules to get enough energy to break their hydrogen bonds to turn from a liquid to a gas. Chemists call this temperature the **boiling point**, the point at which a liquid becomes a gas.

Acetone has a much lower boiling point than water because it takes much less energy to break the weaker intermolecular forces and change the liquid into gas. Acetone boils at 133°F (56°C). This temperature gives the acetone molecules enough energy to break the dipole-dipole bonds and evaporate. Because the boiling point temperature of acetone is lower than that of water, acetone evaporates faster than water.

Additionally, acetone has a strong odor. Because acetone easily evaporates, it is constantly releasing molecules into the air. Human noses can detect the acetone molecules in the air.

Intermolecular forces aren't the only factor involved in evaporation and condensation. Air pressure is another important factor. The lower the air pressure, the less energy molecules need to change from liquid to gas. Think of air pressure as a weight on the surface of a liquid, holding molecules in place. When that weight is heavy (the air pressure is high), liquid molecules need a lot of energy to change to gases. When that weight is light (the air pressure is low), liquid molecules need less energy to change to gases.

SURFACE TENSION

Within a liquid, molecules are surrounded by other molecules. Each molecule exerts an intermolecular force of attraction on surrounding molecules. The molecular force exerted by each molecule is equal in all directions.

On the surface of a liquid, things are different. Molecules at the surface of a liquid are exposed to the air and do not feel the same intermolecular forces from this direction. There is no "pull" or attraction toward the air on these surface molecules. The intermolecular forces from molecules within the liquid, however, pull the surface molecules toward themselves (that is, toward the liquid inside of the container). As a result, intermolecular forces on the surface molecules are not equal, as they are on the molecules within the liquid. This situation creates a strong force, or tension, on the surface of the liquid. Chemists call this *surface tension*.

A similar situation occurs when you suck air through a straw to pick up a small piece of paper. The force created to suck the air is enough to create a "sticky" surface on the end of the straw. Similarly, the force of the molecules within the liquid that pulls on the surface molecules is enough to create a tough, tense layer on the surface of the liquid.

The surface tension of water is so strong that you can actually float a paper clip on the surface of water in a cup (if you're careful). The surface tension will actually support the weight of the paper clip.

Again, take the boiling point of water as an example. Most people live at sea level where air pressure is fairly constant. At sea level, water boils at 212°F (100°C). But the city of Denver, Colorado, is 5,200 ft (1,600 m) above sea level and consequently, has less air pressure. In Denver, water boils at just 203°F (95°C) because there is less air pressure holding the liquid molecules in place.

SWEAT—A PROCESS OF EVAPORATION

All humans sweat. In fact, all mammals—including dogs, horses, and chimpanzees—sweat in one way or another. Sweating, or perspiring, is the body's way of regulating its own temperature and scent, using the process of evaporation.

When humans sweat, we produce a watery, salty, sometimes odorous fluid, through specialized glands in the skin. A **gland** is an organ that creates and releases special substances, including hormones and other liquids. Humans have two types of sweat glands. Both use evaporation, but each gland has a different purpose.

The entire surface of the human body is covered with eccrine sweat glands, with especially high concentrations in the palms of the hands, the soles of the feet, and the forehead. **Eccrine sweat glands** produce and release sweat to regulate the temperature of the body.

When we sweat, water evaporates from the surface of the skin. Because it takes a lot of energy (heat) for water to change from the liquid phase to the gas phase, when sweat evaporates, it actually takes some energy (heat) away from the body. This is what scientists call an **endothermic reaction**. An endothermic reaction absorbs energy.

During the process, the liquid water molecules absorb enough energy (heat) from the body or the surrounding air to break its hydrogen bonds and become a gas. Then the water molecules evaporate, entering the air and taking its extra energy (heat) with it. In the end, this process takes heat away from the body, producing a cooling effect.

Figure 4.2 **As the perspiration on this athlete evaporates, the athlete will feel cooler because evaporation is an endothermic reaction. Evaporating sweat absorbs heat from her body.**

While eccrine sweat glands use evaporation to cool the body, **apocrine sweat glands** use evaporation primarily to emit an odor or scent. Apocrine sweat glands produce fatty, odor-heavy liquids in the armpits and around the genital areas of humans. When sweat evaporates from these areas, the scents are carried into the air as gases.

In humans, odor from sweat glands isn't always desirable (though some may argue this point in certain circumstances). But in nature, animal-specific odors produced by evaporation serve as a means of personal identification. Many animals, including humans, can recognize each other by these individualized scents.

FOG—A PROCESS OF CONDENSATION

On a chilly morning you walk through the streets, perhaps to catch a bus or to get to school, you may notice that it's hard to see objects in front of you. That's because fog has formed overnight.

Fog is actually a cloud formation. The unique thing about fog is that it forms at or near the ground. Just like all clouds, fog forms as the result of condensation.

One type of fog usually occurs at night or early morning, when humidity is relatively high. When the temperature falls, the moisture in the air condenses to form water droplets in the form of fog at or near ground level. Other types of fog occur on the upsides of mountains, over lakes and rivers, and along coastlines.

THE RANGE OF CHANGES

We are most familiar with the melting of ice and the boiling and freezing of liquid water. These phase changes happen all around us. But the melting, boiling, and freezing points of other substances come in quite a range—from super-hot to super-cold. Here are just a few critical temperatures for phase changes of some other common substances.

TABLE 4.1 EXAMPLES OF BOILING POINT AND MELTING OR FREEZING POINT

SUBSTANCE	TEMPERATURE WHEN IT BECOMES A GAS (BOILING POINT)	TEMPERATURE WHEN IT BECOMES A LIQUID (MELTING POINT) OR A SOLID (FREEZING POINT)
Water	212°F (100°C)	32°F (0°C)
Alcohol (ethanol)	172°F (78°C)	−272°F (169°C)
Wax	about 700°F (371°C)	about 137°F (57°C)
Salt	2,669°F (1,465°C)	1,474°F (801°C)
Gold	5,085°F (2,807°C)	1,947°F (1,064°C)
Stainless steel	N/A	2,781°F (1,527°C)
Diamond	8,721°F (4,827°C)	6,422°F (3,550°C)

Melting and Freezing

Melting occurs when a solid changes to a liquid. Freezing is the opposite of melting. It is the process by which a liquid changes to a solid.

Anyone who has eaten an ice cream cone on a hot summer afternoon is familiar with melting. Ice cream drips, popsicles liquefy, and ice cubes slowly melt in a glass of water. Likewise, anyone who has filled an ice cube tray with water and placed it in a freezer knows something about freezing. We take advantage of frozen water to cool our drinks and food, and even to glide on with ice skates.

Not surprisingly, exactly when something melts or freezes is almost entirely dependent on temperature. Unlike some of the other phase changes, pressure plays a much lesser role in melting and freezing. It is temperature, the amount of energy contained in a solid or liquid, that is most crucial.

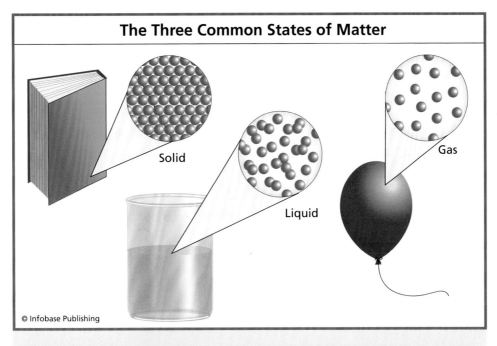

The Three Common States of Matter

Solid

Liquid

Gas

© Infobase Publishing

Figure 5.1   The particles within a solid are packed closer together than particles in a liquid or gas.

When molecules that make up a solid get enough energy to overcome the forces holding them in place, the solid melts into a liquid. Similarly, when the molecules that make up a liquid lose enough energy and slow down, the liquid freezes to form a solid. This chapter takes a closer look at the energy and forces affecting molecules in solids and how they change during melting and freezing.

THE ENERGY OF MOLECULES IN A SOLID

The particles in a solid have less energy than those in gases or liquids, but they still have some energy. As in any state of matter, this energy translates into the ability of these particles to move. Even in a solid—the most tightly packed, organized, and rigid state of matter—the particles are constantly moving.

In the case of solids, the particles are not flowing freely from place to place. Instead, they vibrate inside the structure of the solid. Each particle has its own defined space within a solid. Within that space, each particle that makes up the solid vibrates back and forth, and up and down. Even when a solid appears entirely still and rigid, like a rock or concrete, its particles are moving. The movements are just too small to see under normal conditions.

How fast or slow the particles that make up a solid vibrate depends on the amount of energy they contain. That energy is measured in terms of temperature, or average kinetic energy, of the solid. Particles vibrate slowly when a solid is cold and quickly when a solid is warm. If the temperature of the solid increases to a

TUNGSTEN

The element with the highest melting point is tungsten. This hard, heavy, gray metal will not melt until its temperature reaches 6,192°F (3,422°C).

This unique property makes tungsten a good metal to use when making materials that are used at high temperatures. Light bulb filaments are made of tungsten. Some materials used to build spacecraft, airplane engines, and welding instruments are made entirely of tungsten, because the metal resists heat and stays strong.

Most recently, tungsten has been used to make jewelry. It is often used to make sturdy, long-lasting wedding bands. Perhaps wedding bands are made of tungsten because its durability is symbolic of the state of matrimony. Tungsten is so hard that tungsten jewelry never scratches or needs polishing. Jewelry made of tungsten is clearly in no danger of melting.

certain point, the particles may gain enough energy to break free of their fixed position and flow freely as a liquid. (The properties of the particles remain the same even though the state of matter has changed.) Conversely, when particles that make up a liquid lose enough energy, they no longer flow freely, and the molecular structure takes on a fixed position.

The temperature at which a solid becomes a liquid is known as the **melting point** of the solid. Some solids melt at relatively low temperatures. Ice melts at or above 32°F (0°C). Other solids require higher temperatures to melt. Solid gold, for example, melts at almost 2,000°F (1,100°C).

Not surprisingly, the melting point of a substance is the same as its freezing point (because freezing is the opposite of melting). While water melts at or above 32°F (0°C), it freezes at or below that same temperature. In many cases, chemists use the term "melting point" more often than the term "freezing point," but the two terms really mean the same thing.

As in other phase changes, how a solid turns to a liquid, or liquid turns to a solid, depends on the forces holding the particles together. Strong forces will require higher melting points to form liquids, while weak forces will need less energy. Although chemists group solids into categories based on the different forces holding them together, there are really just two ways to melt a solid: changing ionic bonds or changing covalent bonds, the forces holding solids together.

THE FORCES IN SOLIDS

There can be slightly different forces holding particles together within a solid. Ionic solids, metallic solids, network atomic solids, molecular solids, and amorphous solids each use a different force or combination of forces to hold molecules or atoms together.

Within a solid, there are really only three ways that forces are created between particles: electrons are gained, electrons are lost, or electrons are shared. Forces created when electrons are gained or lost are called *ionic bonds*. Forces created when electrons are shared between atoms are called *covalent bonds*.

Ionic and covalent bonds are important when it comes to melting, because solids change state differently depending on the type of force holding their particles together. Each type of solid has its own melting and freezing process and properties.

Changing Ionic Bonds

When a solid formed with ionic bonds melts, the ionic bonds are actually broken and the particles rearrange themselves in the newly formed liquid. When a liquid freezes, new ionic bonds are actually formed within the solid.

An ionic bond occurs when an atom gains an electron from another atom, or when an atom loses an electron to another atom. Remember that the atom that loses an electron loses a negative charge and becomes a positive cation. The atom that gains an electron receives an extra negative charge and becomes a negative anion.

The attraction between the cation and the anion creates a strong force that holds ions together. The positive and negative ends of ions are bonded together tightly, but they are still in motion. This energy allows the cation and anion to vibrate inside a solid.

As the temperature of the solid goes up, the cations and anions gain more energy. They vibrate more and more as they absorb more energy. When the melting point is reached, the energy of motion is greater than the energy attracting the cations and anions to one another, and ionic bonds are broken. The ions separate and move freely as a liquid.

As the temperature of a liquid goes down, free-flowing cations and anions lose much of their energy and slow their movements. As the liquid loses more heat, the energy of attraction between the cations and anions becomes stronger than the energy of motion, and the charged particles join to form new ionic bonds. If enough ionic bonds form and the temperature is low enough, an ionic solid forms.

Because the force of ionic bonds is quite strong, melting and freezing is not as easy as it sounds. Solids containing ionic bonds typically have very high melting points, because it takes a lot of energy to overcome the force of attraction between cations and anions.

When an ionic solid melts into a liquid, the liquid contains many free-floating cations and anions. These charged particles give the liquid a unique property: the ability to conduct electricity. The cations and anions can move around to "carry" an electrical charge through the liquid. These liquids are known as good conductors.

Changing Covalent Bonds

A covalent bond occurs when two atoms, both in need of electrons to become stable, share electrons that are usually from their outermost energy shells. Instead of one atom giving an electron to another atom, the atoms overlap and share electrons still bound to its nucleus. When a solid formed with covalent bonds melts or freezes, the strength of the covalent bonds that form the molecules are overcome by the strength of the intermolecular forces.

A covalent bond creates a very strong force that holds individual atoms tightly together to form a molecule. These covalently bonded molecules can be held together in a solid by intermolecular forces. When the solid is heated, the covalently bonded molecules are not affected, but the intermolecular forces between molecules changes.

As the temperature of the solid goes up, each molecule gains more and more energy. When the energy of individual molecules is greater than the intermolecular forces holding them together as a solid, the individual molecules break free and the solid becomes a liquid.

As the temperature of the liquid goes down, each molecule loses more and more energy. When the energy of individual molecules is less than the intermolecular forces holding the molecules together in the liquid, the intermolecular forces take over. As the temperature drops, the molecules move less and less and the liquid becomes a solid.

Because intermolecular forces are relatively weak, breaking them doesn't take that much energy. Unlike solids containing ionic bonds, covalently bonded solids tend to have low melting points.

Liquids formed from covalently bonded solids are different from ionic-bond solids in another way as well. Covalently bonded liquids do not contain free-floating charged particles. Instead, they contain tightly-bonded, self-contained, neutral molecules. As a result, a liquid produced from a covalently bonded solid does not conduct electricity well at all. These liquids are good insulators.

FROSTBITE

Frostbite occurs when human skin freezes. It is more likely to happen to the hands, feet, nose and ears, but any bit of skin exposed to severe cold temperatures for long periods of time can suffer from frostbite. The skin gets hard, pale, and cold, but it doesn't hurt once frozen. The pain comes when the skin begins to thaw and feeling returns to the body part. Tingling, burning pains, and red blisters are not uncommon.

To treat frostbite or suspected frostbite, slowly warm the body part and give the person warm fluids to replenish any liquids lost to freezing. If the body part cannot be kept warm once thawed, it is best to wait until constant warmth can be assured. Freezing and refreezing a body part can do even more damage.

In severe cases of frostbite, underlying tissue and blood vessels may freeze as well. If this happens, tissues, muscles, nerves, or bones may be permanently damaged. In severe cases, the affected body part may need to be amputated.

Figure 5.2   Snapping turtles bury themselves in soft mud to hibernate during the winter. Their body processes slow down and they take in oxygen through their skin.

"STORING" THINGS IN NATURE

Melting and freezing are phase changes that don't happen naturally very often because they tend to require a lot of energy. Unlike evaporation and condensation that happen all the time in nature, melting and freezing are reserved for more unique occasions. (Snow, however, is an exception.) In many cases, melting and freezing are used to store things in nature including water on Earth, gases on other planets, and fish in frozen rivers.

Have you ever wondered what happens to the animals in frozen rivers and lakes during the winter? Long ago, scientists used to think marine animals were able to freeze in winter and thaw in summer, but today we know this is not the case. Many fish and turtles, for example, have developed ways to avoid freezing while "storing" themselves over the winter in near-frozen environments.

Take the common snapping turtle (*Chelydra serpentina*) as an example. This large, freshwater turtle lives throughout southern Canada and the Northeastern United States, where winter temperatures can easily drop well below freezing. In the winter, when their ponds start to freeze, these turtles go into hibernation. Like any other substance that becomes very cold, all the molecules and parts inside the turtle slow down to minimal movements.

The turtle's heart only beats once every few minutes, and there is virtually no movement in the body. The turtle doesn't need to eat, and it breathes through specialized skin cells that suck oxygen out of the water. The turtle isn't technically frozen, because no rearrangement of ionic and covalent bonds occurs, but it is as close to being frozen as possible. It is nature's way of helping life forms to adapt to cold conditions.

Sublimation and Deposition

Sublimation occurs when a solid changes directly into a gas. Deposition is the opposite of sublimation. It occurs when a gas changes into a solid. In both of these phase changes, the liquid state of matter is skipped altogether. Instead of a solid melting into a liquid and then becoming a gas, as is more common, the solid skips directly to the gaseous state and vice versa.

Dry ice is perhaps the most common example of sublimation in everyday life. You may have seen this smoking white chunk of "ice" in a Halloween party punch or at a magic show with special effects. Deposition occurs in nature when cold temperatures freeze gaseous water vapors in the air directly into solid ice crystals commonly called frost.

Sublimation and deposition happen only at very low temperatures and pressures, below what scientists call the **triple point**. The triple point is the temperature and pressure at which the solid, liquid, and gas forms of one type of matter are all equally possible. Because the low temperatures and pressures of most triple points are not common in everyday life, these phase changes do not happen very often on Earth.

This chapter takes a closer look at the energy of molecules in gases, the forces they exert, and how they change during sublimation and deposition.

THE ENERGY OF MOLECULES IN A GAS

Gas molecules have a lot of energy. This allows them to move fast and overcome any forces between molecules that might cause them to slow down. Unlike liquid molecules that transfer a lot of energy when they collide, collisions between gas molecules are elastic. An elastic collision is one where molecules collide but the total amount of energy stays the same. Some gas molecules have high energy; some gas molecules have low energy. When gas molecules collide, they transfer energy among each other constantly.

Gas molecules are always moving. They possess kinetic energy, or energy of motion. Temperature, of course, is one key to the energy level of individual gas molecules. The kinetic energy of a gas depends on the temperature of that gas. By raising the temperature of a gas in a closed container, you raise the kinetic energy of that gas, which increases the speed of the molecules. By decreasing the temperature of a gas, you decrease the kinetic energy of that gas, slowing the molecules traveling in the container.

As gases are heated, they expand—the molecules get farther and farther apart as the temperature goes up. Cooled gases condense—the molecules get closer and closer together as the temperature goes down. When the temperature gets low enough, the gas molecules draw close enough together and slow down enough so that intermolecular forces start to take hold. The gas condenses to form a liquid. In reverse, by adding enough heat, the liquid evaporates to form a gas.

The sublimation and deposition phase changes occur when the effects of temperature are combined with pressure. Because gas molecules have a lot of energy, they constantly travel quickly in straight lines until they hit something. When the gas molecules hit the sides of the container in which they are held in, they exert pressure on the container's sides.

MEASURING PRESSURE

A barometer is an instrument that measures air pressure. Traditional barometers used a long, enclosed vertical glass tube containing mercury. The open end of the tube was placed in a bowl of mercury. The weight of the air on the surface of the mercury caused the liquid to travel up the tube until the pressure of the column of mercury

Figure 6.1   A modern barometer uses the same principles as mercury barometers to measure air pressure.

equaled the pressure of the air on the bowl. The length of the mercury column gave a reading of air pressure.

Many modern barometers use different materials (mercury is known to be highly toxic to humans) but work in basically the same way. These instruments are often used in weather prediction to distinguish high-and-low pressure weather systems. A high-air pressure system means good weather is coming; while a low-air pressure system means storms are more likely.

Not surprisingly, the size of the container affects the gas pressure. Gas molecules expand or contract to fit any container—a bottle, a box, a room, or an atmosphere. In general, gas molecules stay far apart from each other, leaving lots of space between molecules. But the amount of space between molecules varies depending on the size of the container.

Imagine that there are 100 gas molecules contained in a room. Now take those 100 gas molecules and pack them, or compress them, into a soda bottle. Gases are compressible. In this smaller container, those 100 gas molecules have a lot less space to move around than they did in the room. The fast-moving molecules will hit the sides of the bottle much more often than the walls of the room, increasing the gas pressure within the soda bottle. If the soda bottle gets smaller—really small for the number of molecules present—the gas will become a liquid or, at a very low temperature, a solid. When the gas changes directly into a solid, deposition occurs.

THE FORCES IN GASES

Unlike liquids and solids, there are no forces holding molecules together in a gas. In fact, gas molecules are not particularly attracted to each other at all. The only thing that holds gas molecules together is the shape of the container around them (In the atmosphere, gases surround Earth due to Earth's gravity.). The behavior of molecules in that container is not dependent on any special forces between atoms or molecules. Instead, temperature and pressure are the most important factors.

During condensation, gaseous particles slow down and are overcome by the intermolecular forces at work in liquids. During sublimation and deposition, temperature and pressure conditions are so extreme that the liquid phase simply gets skipped.

Imagine you took those 100 gas molecules floating in a room and packed them into a very small space, such as the space inside a single grain of salt. Here, the pressure inside the grain would be so great that the molecules would be forced into very close contact with each other.

In some substances, compression of this sort would lead to condensation, forcing the molecules to interact with each other much like the molecules in a liquid. This pressure-process of condensation can also produce something called **supercritical fluids**, liquids that don't behave like normal liquids and instead have properties of both liquids and gases.

In other substances, the molecules would be forced to interact with each other much like the molecules in a solid interact. Extreme pressure can force molecules to organize as they would in a rigid solid without ever becoming a liquid. Only when both the temperature and pressure are extremely low, below the triple point of a substance, does this occur.

The triple point of any given substance is easiest to identify from a phase diagram. A **phase diagram** shows the state of matter of a given material under all possible temperatures and pressures. Temperature is listed along the horizontal, or x-axis, of the plot, while pressure is listed along the vertical, or y-axis, of the plot (Figure 6.2).

Given a certain temperature and pressure, the chart shows what state of matter will exist for that substance. Phase diagrams mark the triple point of a substance with the letter "A." Below this "A," the solid, liquid, and gaseous phases of a substance can all exist. To change between the phases requires only tiny changes to temperature and pressure.

The triple points for most substances do not occur under normal conditions. Take water as an example. The temperature of water's triple point is nothing unusual—just above the freezing point. But the pressure of water's triple point is extremely low— 0.006 atmospheres—a level that exists only in outer space.

At the triple point pressure, liquid water cannot exist without a change in temperature. Instead, heated ice skips the liquid stage and changes directly from a solid to a gas in the sublimation phase

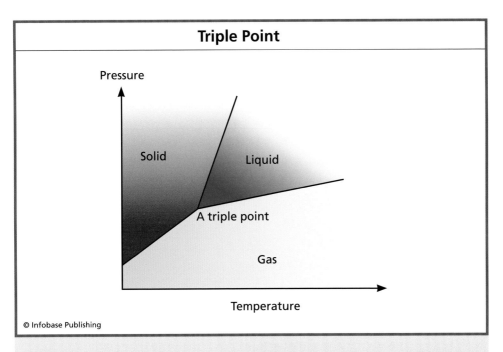

Triple Point

© Infobase Publishing

Figure 6.2 At the triple point, a certain substance can exist as a solid, liquid, or gas. A slight change in pressure or temperature can change the state of matter of the substance.

change. When cooled, water vapor skips the liquid stage and freezes into ice in the deposition phase change.

SUBLIMATION AND DEPOSITION IN ACTION

Sublimation and deposition of most molecules does not usually occur on Earth. Scientists can make these phase changes occur in laboratories under controlled conditions, but they are rarely useful or practical.

However, one common molecule does undergo sublimation and deposition on Earth: carbon dioxide. Carbon dioxide (CO_2) is present in the atmosphere as a gas and exists as a solid known as dry ice.

The sublimation of dry ice occurs constantly at normal temperature and pressure, producing carbon dioxide gas. As molecules in the solid gain energy, their increased movement is enough to break out of the solid phase. But because liquid carbon dioxide forms only at extremely low pressures, a block of dry ice melting on Earth sublimes directly to the gaseous phase.

Deposition of carbon dioxide gas occurs only with some help from humans. Carbon dioxide gas is compressed with pressure into a liquid and cooled. Then the liquid is allowed to expand at normal pressures. This expansion happens so quickly that much energy, or

SUPERCRITICAL CARBON DIOXIDE

Supercritical carbon dioxide is carbon dioxide that exists at a very high temperature and pressure. Under these conditions, carbon dioxide becomes a supercritical fluid, taking on some of the properties of both a gas and a liquid. For human purposes, supercritical carbon dioxide works well as a solvent.

A solvent is a fluid that dissolves solids, liquids, and gases, breaking them down into their separate parts. Many solvents are used in cleaners and detergents to separate or remove unwanted substances. Chemical solvents are quite useful and widely used, but many are considered toxic or bad for the environment.

Supercritical carbon dioxide is considered a "green" solvent because it is made of nothing more than carbon dioxide, a substance naturally present on Earth. Currently, supercritical carbon dioxide is used to decaffeinate coffee beans, extract new scents for perfume, and clean clothes.

Figure 6.3 The water vapor formed around dry ice is often used for dramatic effects.

heat, is lost and some of the carbon dioxide gas freezes into snow-like crystals. These snow pieces are then packed together in a block known as dry ice.

Dry ice seems to have two main purposes: to keep things cold and to create dramatic effects. Because the temperature of frozen carbon dioxide is so cold, about –109°F (–79°C), it is often used to keep food and beverages cold when ordinary refrigeration is not available. At the same time, a block of dry ice constantly emits a thick, white, fog-like vapor often used for its special effects value.

But the carbon dioxide gas coming off a block of dry ice is actually clear and colorless. When this cold gas interacts with the water vapor naturally present in air, another phase change takes over. The cold temperatures make the water vapor in the air condense into a liquid—and this is what produces the thick, white, fog-like vapor so valued for its eerie look and feel.

Other States
of Matter

Solids, liquids, and gases are the three states of matter tradi-
tionally recognized in chemistry. But more recently, some
scientists have argued that other states of matter exist as well. Each
"new" state of matter is some variation of the original three, but
some states are more readily accepted by scientists than others.
This chapter looks at a handful of other states of matter.

Plasmas and Bose-Einstein condensates are relatively well-
accepted as the fourth and fifth states of matter, while the others described here are more controversial. These are sometimes
considered other states of matter and sometimes viewed as special
categories of traditional solids, liquids, and gases.

THE FOURTH STATE OF MATTER: PLASMA

Plasma is an ionized, or charged, gas. Like a traditional gas, plasma
has no defined shape or volume and disperses to fill the shape of

its container. Likewise, the molecules and atoms are far apart, fast-moving, and not organized in any particular way.

Because of these similarities with traditional gases, some consider plasma its own special category of gases, not a separate state of matter. But the similarities stop here. The more scientists learn about plasma and its unique qualities, the more it is widely considered to be its own state of matter. (Note in this case, the state of matter plasma is completely unrelated to blood plasma.)

Energy in Plasmas

At the molecular level, plasmas have more energy than any other state of matter. This energy comes from heat, electricity in the atmosphere, or light in space. It gives some of the electrons orbiting atoms and molecules in plasmas enough energy to break away from their original nuclei and float freely in the gas. These free-floating electrons make the gas ionized (charged) and are responsible for many of the unique properties of plasmas.

For starters, the electrons enable plasmas to conduct electricity well. The charged particles in the gas can carry other charges with them as they move, allowing electricity to pass through plasmas with ease. This strong conductivity then allows plasmas to act and react as electric and magnetic fields.

An **electric field** is the space surrounding a charged particle that exerts a force on other particles. In plasmas, the space surrounding the moving electrons exerts a force on other particles to create an electric field. A **magnetic field** is something that exerts a force on other moving, charged particles. In plasmas, the negatively charged electrons can exert a force on other moving particles. When this happens, the plasma is said to be magnetized.

Despite the ability of plasma to act as an electric and magnetic field, any plasma itself is considered to be electrically neutral. There are about as many negatively charged electrons as there are positively charged ions (left over when the electrons separate from

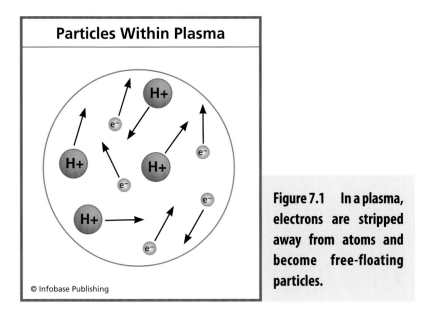

Particles Within Plasma

© Infobase Publishing

Figure 7.1 In a plasma, electrons are stripped away from atoms and become free-floating particles.

atoms and the gas became ionized) inside a plasma to render it neutral to other things.

Beyond these general properties, the characteristics of individual plasmas depend on the temperature and density of each ionized gas. There are a lot of different types of plasmas. In fact, they are the most common state of matter in the universe.

Where Plasmas Are Found

Plasmas were first identified and described by scientists in the late 1800s, but they didn't get their name until 1928. In some ways, it's interesting that it took this long to identify plasmas, because much of the volume of the universe is considered plasma.

Some experts estimate more than 99 percent of the visible universe is made of plasma.[10] The Sun, stars, and all the space in between are different types of plasma. Lightning and lightning balls are types of plasma. Even the spaces between galaxies in the solar system are filled with plasmas.

To get a feel for the range of temperatures and densities of different plasmas, compare a star to the Aurora Borealis (or Northern

Lights) seen shimmering in the sky above the North Pole. Stars are extremely large, hot, dense, balls of plasma. Large stars have an immense gravitational pull and can have surface temperatures up to 50,000 K (almost 90,000°F).

The Aurora Borealis, on the other hand, is a stream of cooling plasma leaving the surface of the Sun and colliding with other gases in the atmosphere of our planet. When it leaves the Sun, the temperature of the plasma stream is only about 6,200 Kelvin (11,000°F). It is comparatively cool and much less dense than a star.

FUSION POWER

Fusion power is a method of creating energy by fusing the nuclei of atoms together. During this process, called nuclear fusion, the nuclei of two or more atoms combine into one nucleus. The final nucleus actually ends up with less mass than the sum of the original nuclei. The "lost" mass is converted into energy.

While it takes a lot of energy to make atoms combine, the process actually releases more energy than it takes to make it happen. It is an exothermic reaction. To make nuclei combine, they must collide with more energy than they have holding themselves together. The forces in a nucleus are stronger than any type of intermolecular force or chemical bond, so it takes a lot of energy to force a fusion of nuclei together.

In nature, these collisions only occur with the needed force inside high-energy plasmas, mainly in stars. The core of a star is a nuclear fusion power-house that uses intense heat to combine the nuclei of hydrogen atoms into helium atoms. When combinations occur, the energy is emitted as light. It is the light from nuclear fusion reactions that we see as bright stars in the night sky.

On Earth, scientists are studying plasmas as a source for nuclear fusion reactions. In theory, if we can understand how to make atoms combine nuclei in controlled conditions, we can produce large amounts of energy that could be used to make electricity.

On Earth, humans use plasmas for different purposes. In fluorescent lights, electricity is used to excite mercury gas to the plasma state, where the high-energy electrons emit light. In neon lights, electricity is used to excite neon or argon gas to the plasma state, emitting colorful light. Plasma televisions are made of two glass panels with certain kinds of gases contained between. Electricity is used to excite the gases to the plasma state to create visible light.

THE FIFTH STATE OF MATTER: BOSE-EINSTEIN CONDENSATES

A **Bose-Einstein condensate (BEC)** is a super-cold, super-slow moving, clump of atoms. In a sense, BECs are the opposite of plasmas. While plasmas are super-excited, high-energy gases, BECs are super-slow, low-energy liquids. Unlike plasmas, which exist naturally throughout the universe, BECs do not exist under natural conditions.

Energy in BECs

The trick to making a BEC in the laboratory is temperature. This state of matter exists only at super-low temperatures near absolute zero. At **absolute zero** (O K, −459°F) all molecular motion stops and there is no heat energy left in a substance. In the laboratory, scientists can create temperatures just a few billionths of a degree above absolute zero.

At such cold temperatures, atoms start to do strange things. This state of matter is called a *condensate* because it is formed by a sort of condensation of atoms. Under normal temperatures, atoms exist in their own bit of space. Near absolute zero, these atoms condense and clump together and form what scientists call a super atom.

Not surprisingly, these super atoms give rise to some unusual properties of BECs, many of which are not entirely understood. One of the most interesting properties is the ability of these liquids to spontaneously flow out of their containers.

BECs exist in their lowest energy state. That is, it's simply not possible for them to lose any more energy, even by bumping into things—including the sides of their containers. A normal liquid stays within its container because when its molecules bump up against the sides, they lose some energy. This energy loss is enough to make gravity the dominant force on the liquid. Gravity holds the liquid within its container. BECs are different.

Since BECs have no more energy to lose, bumping up against the sides of the container does not take energy away. Instead, the molecules in BECs are attracted to the molecules making up the sides of their container. This attraction, or adhesion, is strong enough to overcome the force of gravity. Since adhesion is the dominant force in this case, BECs will spontaneously spill out of their container and collect all around the outside.

If such spillage does not happen in a controlled, near-absolute zero environment, the BEC will simply vaporize back into a gas and disappear. Near-absolute zero temperatures do not exist in nature and are difficult to create in the laboratory. But it can be done.

Where BECs Are Found

Albert Einstein first predicted the existence of BECs in 1925 while studying the physics of atoms and the work of Indian scientist Satyendra Nath Bose. But at the time, Einstein did not have the technology needed to create BECs.

Seventy years later, in 1995, two scientists at the University of Colorado at Boulder, Eric Cornell and Carl Wieman, created the first known BEC in a laboratory using light and magnets.

Laser lights blasted at atoms act like hail storms. Tiny packages of light, called photons, bombard the atoms from all directions like hail. Eventually, the force of the photons makes the atoms slow down and nearly stop. At the same time, magnets draw the higher energy atoms away, leaving only the slow-moving atoms. Over time, if enough slow-moving atoms are collected, they condense into what we call a BEC.

SATYENDRA NATH BOSE

While most of us are familiar with the name Albert Einstein, few Americans have likely heard of Satyendra Nath Bose. Together, Bose and Einstein envisioned what is now known as Bose-Einstein condensation using math. They developed a foundation of statistics supporting its existence, even though they could never prove it.

Figure 7.2   Satyendra Nath Bose

Bose was born in Calcutta, India, and appeared to lead a fairly unglorious life. He had a family, attended good schools, and worked as a college lecturer at universities in India.

At the time, Bose could not get his research paper about his experimental observations of microscopic particles published because it contained a math error. At first, Bose thought this error was an honest mistake. But because the calculation agreed with his observations, he began to think it was not a mistake at all. Rather, it was an indication that scientific thinking of the time about microscopic particles was wrong.

Research journals refused to publish the paper with the mathematical error and did not accept Bose's alternative explanation that science was wrong. Perhaps out of frustration, Bose sent his paper to Albert Einstein, who immediately saw the significance of Bose's idea. Einstein wrote his own paper to accompany and support Bose's and sent both to a prestigious research journal where they were published in 1924.

Because BECs are so hard to make and maintain, and because all their properties are not yet understood, there have not yet been many commercial uses for this state of matter. It is largely used by scientists in the laboratory to study quantum mechanics, the study of atoms and subatomic particles.

SOMETIMES STATES OF MATTER

The definition of *state of matter* isn't as rigid as it may seem. Some substances simply don't fit squarely in one category or another, and they don't have to be an obscure substance either. What is the state of matter of mayonnaise, for example? It's sort of a solid, but also, sort of a liquid.

These unclear substances tend to generate some debate among scientists. Some consider these in-between phases merely as alternate forms of solids, liquids, and gases. Others prefer to classify them as entirely separate states of matter.

While plasmas and Bose-Einstein condensates are widely accepted as "new" states of matter, a few phases are still very much on the fringe. These substances do not fit squarely in the traditional states of matter categories and are described here.

Liquid Crystals

Liquid crystals are something between a liquid and a solid. The molecules in liquid crystals are arranged in structured, crystal-like patterns, but are able to flow and move like liquids. Scientists groups liquid crystals into categories depending on how molecules are oriented.

Humans use liquid crystals in a variety of ways. The *LCD* in popular LCD monitors stands for "liquid crystal display." Each dot of color in these displays is light passing through a thin layer of liquid crystals. When electricity passes through the layer, the liquid crystal structure is turned and twisted to reflect different colors of light. LCD monitors are particularly popular because they take low amounts of energy to operate.

Figure 7.3 LCD displays are used in many common objects.

Nature also uses liquid crystals. The protein solution, or silk, spun by spiders to make webs is actually a type of liquid crystal. The well-known strength of the web depends on the crystal structure of the molecules in the liquid silk.

Cell membranes, the protective layers that surround cells in living things, are also made largely of liquid crystals. A cell membrane protects a cell while allowing itself to flow and stretch as needed.

Superfluids and Supersolids

A **superfluid** is a liquid that will flow endlessly when placed in a closed loop. Some elements, most notably helium (He), become superfluids at temperatures near absolute zero. This phase is considered a second liquid phase and has been known since the late 1930s, but relatively little is understood about it.

A **supersolid** is actually a superfluid with the crystal-like structure of a traditional solid. Inside a supersolid, the atoms are moving and flowing as superfluids, but outside, the substance maintains its shape. Supersolids had been predicted to exist in theory, but were only created in a laboratory in 2004.

8

Phase Changes at Home

Phase changes happen all around us all the time, not only during super-large scale events, as in Earth's water cycle. Take a tour of your home and you will likely find phase changes at work in nearly every room.

We use changing states of matter to make our lives more comfortable. Many modern conveniences found all around us, especially in our homes, rely on the changing state of matter. This chapter takes you on a tour of some of the phase changes all around you.

IN THE AIR

If you live in a place where there is very hot or very cold weather, you might have machinery to help regulate the temperature of the air in your home and car. Air conditioners and certain types of heaters take advantage of the energy released during some state-of-matter changes to adjust temperature.

Air Conditioners

Traditional air conditioners use a continuous cycle of evaporation and condensation to remove heat from a room and blow it outside. To cool the air, a part of the air conditioner contains a gas that naturally evaporates at cold temperatures. This gas is called a refrigerant. The refrigerant flows continuously through three parts of the appliance that change its state of matter from liquid to a gas and back. These parts are a condenser, an evaporator, and a compressor.

In the condenser, the refrigerant changes from a gas to a liquid. This process produces heat, which is usually blown with a fan out the back of the air conditioner to the outside. The purpose of this phase change is to supply the air conditioner with liquid.

The liquid then goes to the evaporator, where two phase changes happen at the same time. The liquid refrigerant expands into a gas, giving off cold air which is blown back into the room to cool the temperature. At the same time, a fan sucks in hot, humid air from inside the room. As the hot, humid air hits the cold air from the gas, it condenses into water droplets.

Finally, the refrigerant gas returns to the condenser through a compressor. The compressor pumps the gas back to the condenser so that the process is continuous. Although a lot happens inside an air conditioner, it is all relatively simple science and requires little maintenance.

Over time, the refrigerant gas may drain out of the system and needs to be replaced, particularly in the air conditioners in cars. Basic window air conditioners tend to use a lot of electricity to operate, but they work well.

An alternative type of air conditioner used in certain areas of the country needs neither refrigerant gas nor lots of electricity to work. These evaporative coolers, or swamp coolers, take advantage of the cooling ability of evaporating water.

The trick is that evaporative coolers only work in very dry, very hot places. These simple machines use a fan to blow warm,

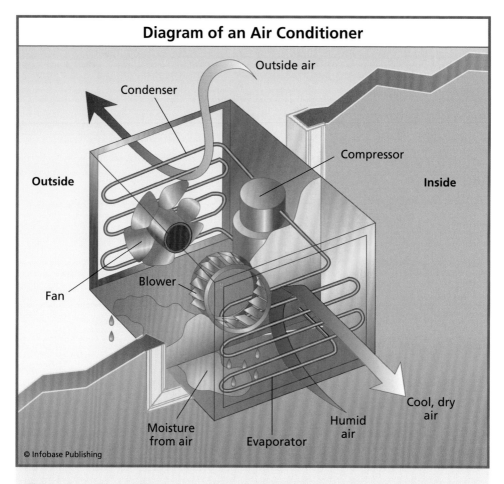

Diagram of an Air Conditioner

Outside air

Condenser

Compressor

Outside

Inside

Fan

Blower

Cool, dry
air

Moisture
from air

Humid
air

Evaporator

© Infobase Publishing

Figure 8.1 Air conditioners use the principles of evaporation and condensation to cool rooms.

outside air across a pad soaked in a pool of water. The heated air causes the liquid water to evaporate to a cool gas, which is blown into the building. This results in a room full of water-heavy, cool air.

There is no need for the condensation part of the cycle because hot air is in continuous supply on warm days. As a result, evaporative coolers use far less energy than traditional refrigerated air conditioners. They are very popular in hot, dry areas of the country where coolers are used nearly year-round.

Heaters

There are many different types of home heaters that work in many different ways. Some use phase changes to produce heat. The sort of heat you use in your home depends a lot on where you live and how cold it gets in the winter.

A heat pump is perhaps the simplest example of a heater that uses phase changes. Often seen in areas with mild winters, a heat pump is nothing more than an air conditioner in reverse. Instead of moving heat from the inside to outside, they move heat from outside to inside.

In winter, there is obviously not a lot of heat outside. But heat pumps extract water vapors from the cold winter air (even cold air still contains some water vapor), and condense it to release heat. The only problem here is the production of water droplets and condensation. These water droplets freeze on the outside of the heat pump and need to be thawed every once in a while.

IN THE LIVING ROOM

Deposition is the phase change responsible for the dust in your living room and throughout the rest of your home. Dust, the tiny particles of dirt and grime ever-present in the atmosphere, is considered an **aerosol**. An aerosol is a tiny piece of solid or liquid suspended in a gas. Aerosols can be just a few molecules stuck together. But when they grow large enough, they change state from a gas to a solid.

Technically, aerosol particles already have a tiny bit of solid or liquid when they float as a gas, so they are not pure gases at the start. When these aerosol particles accumulate, they can lose the high-energy level that makes them a gas in the first place. Deposition takes over and changes the floating aerosols into solids that collect on surfaces in the room.

IN THE BATHROOM

Evaporation and condensation are phase changes at work often in the bathroom. When you take a shower, use a sauna, or dry your hair, you are changing the state of matter of water.

Showers and Saunas

When you take a hot shower, evaporation of the hot water adds water vapor to the air in the room. When those warm water vapors encounter cooler air, probably on the other side of the room from the shower, the vapors condense to form droplets of liquid water on all surfaces.

This process of evaporating shower water and condensing water vapor results in a "foggy" bathroom mirror. The fog on the mirror and other cold surfaces is actually a cloud made of tiny droplets of water.

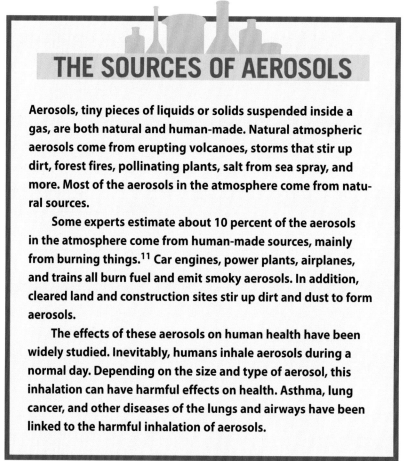

THE SOURCES OF AEROSOLS

Aerosols, tiny pieces of liquids or solids suspended inside a gas, are both natural and human-made. Natural atmospheric aerosols come from erupting volcanoes, storms that stir up dirt, forest fires, pollinating plants, salt from sea spray, and more. Most of the aerosols in the atmosphere come from natural sources.

Some experts estimate about 10 percent of the aerosols in the atmosphere come from human-made sources, mainly from burning things.[11] Car engines, power plants, airplanes, and trains all burn fuel and emit smoky aerosols. In addition, cleared land and construction sites stir up dirt and dust to form aerosols.

The effects of these aerosols on human health have been widely studied. Inevitably, humans inhale aerosols during a normal day. Depending on the size and type of aerosol, this inhalation can have harmful effects on health. Asthma, lung cancer, and other diseases of the lungs and airways have been linked to the harmful inhalation of aerosols.

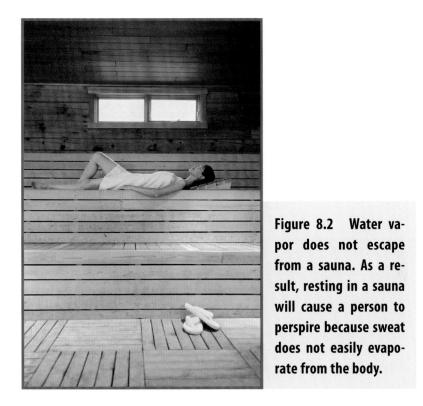

Figure 8.2 Water vapor does not escape from a sauna. As a result, resting in a sauna will cause a person to perspire because sweat does not easily evaporate from the body.

Some homes in cold climates (including Alaska and Finland) have saunas. Saunas come in two varieties: dry and wet. Dry saunas do not use water to create a heated atmosphere. Wet saunas take advantage of water's ability to change state. Inside a wet sauna, evaporation of hot water adds water vapor to the air in the room much like a shower does. But in this case, there is no cold air available in the room to cause that water vapor to condense. Instead, liquid water changes to water vapor and stays in the air.

This extra water vapor in the air makes it harder for humans to utilize their natural evaporative cooling method: sweat. Humans sweat in the intense heat of a sauna, but the sweat cannot evaporate easily because the air is already filled with water vapor. As a result, the human body loses its ability to regulate its own body temperature. This explains why sitting in a sauna can feel extremely warm even when temperatures are not that high.

Hair Dryers

Hair dryers use rapidly moving hot or cold air to accelerate the evaporation of water from hair and make hair dry. The molecules in liquid water on the hair gain energy from the moving air and break away as water vapor. When all the liquid water molecules break away, the hair is dry.

This simple, straightforward phase change allows for a couple of different things: the convenience of quick-drying hair and a range of modern hairstyles.

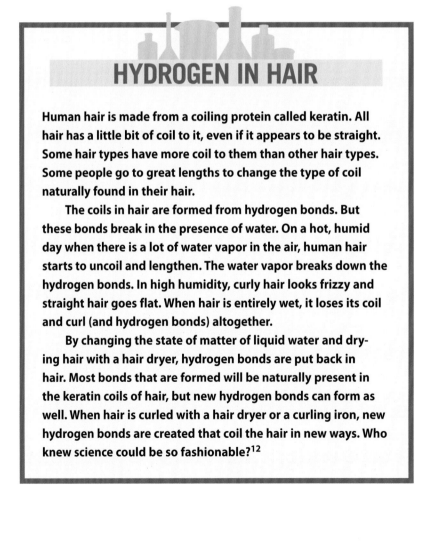

HYDROGEN IN HAIR

Human hair is made from a coiling protein called keratin. All hair has a little bit of coil to it, even if it appears to be straight. Some hair types have more coil to them than other hair types. Some people go to great lengths to change the type of coil naturally found in their hair.

The coils in hair are formed from hydrogen bonds. But these bonds break in the presence of water. On a hot, humid day when there is a lot of water vapor in the air, human hair starts to uncoil and lengthen. The water vapor breaks down the hydrogen bonds. In high humidity, curly hair looks frizzy and straight hair goes flat. When hair is entirely wet, it loses its coil and curl (and hydrogen bonds) altogether.

By changing the state of matter of liquid water and drying hair with a hair dryer, hydrogen bonds are put back in hair. Most bonds that are formed will be naturally present in the keratin coils of hair, but new hydrogen bonds can form as well. When hair is curled with a hair dryer or a curling iron, new hydrogen bonds are created that coil the hair in new ways. Who knew science could be so fashionable?[12]

IN THE KITCHEN

The kitchen is perhaps the most obvious place in a home where phase changes are put to work. The refrigerator, gas stove, and the process of cooking all use phase changes for many purposes.

Refrigerators

A refrigerator works almost exactly like an air conditioner. It uses a condenser, compressor, and evaporator to continuously change the state of matter of a refrigerant gas.

When the gas condenses, it gives off heat and forms a liquid; when the liquid evaporates, it gives off cold and turns back into a gas. The compressor keeps the gas moving through the system and constantly changes the state of the gas. The heat produced during this process dissipates into the air, while the cold is trapped in an insulated box.

That insulated box is where the food is kept. Unlike an air conditioner that blows cold air into a room, a refrigerator traps all the cold air in one place. The cold temperature slows the growth of bacteria in food, allowing leftovers to last for days without going bad.

In the freezer, another phase change is at work storing food over long periods of time. When food is frozen, any bacterial growth in the food completely stops; bacteria become inactive at freezing temperatures. At the same time, the process of freezing changes the state of the matter.

In the case of meat and most vegetables, phase changes in-duced by freezing temperatures are easily reversed with melting or thawing. The liquids and solids in meat freeze and melt without much noticeable affect on taste. Likewise, the liquids and solids in most vegetables can freeze and melt without trouble. But fruit is another story.

Because fruits generally contain large amounts of water, when they freeze the water inside turns to ice and expands. When frozen fruits melt, the thawed liquid shrinks and leaves the fruit mushy and stretched out. Food phase changes are handy, but they don't work in all cases.

Barbecue Grills

People who cook foods using a barbecue may use a type of gas-powered grill. This type of apparatus uses evaporation to change liquid fuel, such as propane, into a gas. The gas is then burned to create the energy used to cook food. In this case, the phase change known as evaporation is the first step. The chemical reaction known as combustion is the second step.

Evaporation is necessary in gas-powered barbecue grills. Fuel is safe and easy to store as a liquid. The liquid fuel is stored under pressure in a tank attached to the barbecue grill. When the grill is turned on, the liquid fuel is heated just enough so it evaporates into a gas. This gas is easily ignited to create a cooking flame.

The process of igniting the flame is called combustion. Combustion is a type of **chemical reaction** that rearranges the elements in fuel to form new molecules. It is fundamentally different than a phase change, which usually just changes the forces and energy between molecules in a substance rather than making new substances.

The process of combustion requires three ingredients: oxygen, fuel, and energy. The liquid fuel powering a gas barbecue grill contains the element carbon. In propane, each propane molecule contains three carbon atoms. When carbon in propane is ignited with a spark, it combines with the oxygen in the air to produce carbon dioxide (CO_2) and a flame. Barbecue grills are designed to allow control over the amount of liquid gas being evaporated and the size of the flame produced.

IN THE GARAGE

It's likely the lights in your garage (or in other rooms of your home) contain a gas that is changed into plasma. Low-energy fluorescent lights, commonly found in the garage, use electricity to excite mercury gas to the plasma state. The new plasma contains lots of free-floating, fast-moving electrons that emit energy as ultraviolet light.

The only problem is that ultraviolet light is not normally visible to the human eye. To rectify this problem, the inside of the light bulb is coated with a fluorescent, often slightly glowing layer full of metals and salts.

This fluorescent layer absorbs the ultraviolet light coming off the plasma and radiates the energy in a different form. The new form is visible light. The blend of metals and salts in the fluorescent layer control the color of the new visible light.

Phase Changes in Industry

Somewhere in between the phase changes happening in your home and the phase changes happening on the planet, are phase changes that take place on an industrial scale. Humans have learned to manipulate phase changes on large, industrial-sized scales to create machines and substances that improve our lives. This chapter examines each type of phase change and how it is used at the industrial level.

EVAPORATION AND CONDENSATION

Steam engines are perhaps the greatest example of a phase change of industrial proportion. Also known as external combustion engines, steam engines boil liquid water to produce gaseous steam (phase change: evaporation). That steam is used to drive moving parts, and the gas is changed back into liquid to be boiled again (phase change: condensation).

Before the steam engine was invented, there were no automatic pumps to draw well water or engines to propel cars or trains. Since their conception in the 1660s, steam engines have evolved, been improved, and, in some cases, even been replaced, but they are still very much a part of industrial society.

Early Steam Engines

The first widely used industrial steam engine, the Watt Steam Engine, invented in 1765, used evaporation and condensation to efficiently create energy. Fire was used to boil water in an enclosed space to produce steam. The Watt Steam Engine was an external combustion engine because of the external source of fuel. In this case, the fire burned outside of the engine itself.

The expanding steam from the boiling water was directed to a cylinder where it pushed on pistons, causing them to move. In the cylinder, the force of the expanding steam drove the pistons up. The pistons, in turn, moved beams or gears to do the work.

As the steam lost energy, it was collected in a separate chamber where it cooled and condensed back into liquid water. In the process of condensing in a sealed chamber, the steam created a **vacuum**, a space empty of matter. This vacuum allowed atmospheric pressure to drive the piston down again, preparing it for another round of work.

In early steam engines, the pistons were connected to large beams. The beams, in turn, were connected to long rods that descended into wells or mines. The rods powered water pumps that slowly moved water up and out of the hole. By the early 1800s, the engines were designed so that the expanding steam moved wheels rather than pistons. This new design was soon used to power steamboats, trains, and early types of automobiles.

Today, boats and trains powered by steam are not widely used. Most transportation steam engines have been replaced by internal combustion engines, which burn fuel inside the engine

Figure 9.1 The Watt Steam Engine (mid 1770s)

itself. Also, the fuel of choice is not wood or coal, but flammable gas.

Steam Power

Not all steam engines are obsolete. The primary industrial use for modern steam engines is in power generation. In fact, steam engines are used to generate more than 80 percent of all electricity produced in the world.[13] Depending on where you live, you may have evaporation and condensation to thank for your electricity.

The type of steam engine used to generate electricity is called a steam turbine. Like a primitive steam engine, a steam turbine heats water to produce steam. The steam is then driven through a series of stages that convert the energy of steam to mechanical energy. Instead of driving simple pistons, steam turbines drive a series of circular blades or rotors. These rotors power electric generators that make electricity. Eventually, the steam is condensed back into the system.

Most of the world's electricity is generated with steam turbines. The major difference between power plants is the type of fuel used to boil the water and change it from liquid to gas. Nuclear power plants use nuclear energy to boil the water in steam turbines, while fossil fuel plants burn fossil fuels, such as coal, to boil the water in steam turbines.

You might get your electricity from a sophisticated nuclear power plant, but it still relies on old-fashioned steam released by the phase change of water.

FREEZING AND SUBLIMATION

The process of freeze-drying food uses freezing and sublimation to preserve food for long periods of time without refrigeration. The goal of freeze-drying food is to remove all of the water from food without using heat. This leaves a completely dry product that has not yet been cooked. Hot water can later be added to rehydrate the food and produce an edible, freshly cooked meal.

The trick is removing the water from food in the right way. If heat is used to evaporate the water from food, the heat inevitably cooks the food so that when the food is rehydrated, it does not have the proper shape and texture. Overall, evaporation doesn't always get all the water out of food anyway; evaporation often leaves five to ten percent of the water behind. The product looks dry, but it is not.

To get the water out of food without using heat, freeze-drying skips the liquid phase of water entirely. First, all the water in food is frozen solid in place. Then sublimation is used to convert the solid water into water vapor so it can be extracted without changing the shape or texture of the food.

Freeze-drying machines first freeze the water in the food completely—the first phase change. Then they use sublimation to change the solid water into water vapor—the second phase change. As you know, during sublimation the molecules in a solid gain

Figure 9.2   The space program supplies astronauts with freeze-dried foods. Many foods, such as shrimp fried rice, can be freeze-dried.

enough energy to break free of their place in the solid's structure. But the pressure is so low that the molecules cannot form a liquid, so they convert directly into a gas.

Freeze-drying machines apply a small amount of heat to a frozen food sealed in a chamber. This heat prompts the molecules in the solid to break free. But at the same time those small amounts of heat are applied, a pump sucks the air out of the chamber and lowers the pressure. The low pressure prevents the liquid phase of water from forming, so the molecules in the solid convert directly to water vapor.

The result is an extremely lightweight, dehydrated food. When sealed in an airtight package, the food can be preserved without any special conditions for many years. Because there is no water, bacteria or other microbial life cannot live in the food; the food is in no danger of spoiling. To be eaten, water is added to recreate the original meal.

While most people may not consume freeze-dried foods, the process is widely used by the federal government. The military freeze-dries meals for troops in battle or abroad. The space industry freeze-dries meals for transport into space and to be consumed aboard spacecraft. More recently, outdoor companies have begun selling freeze-dried food for people to eat while camping.

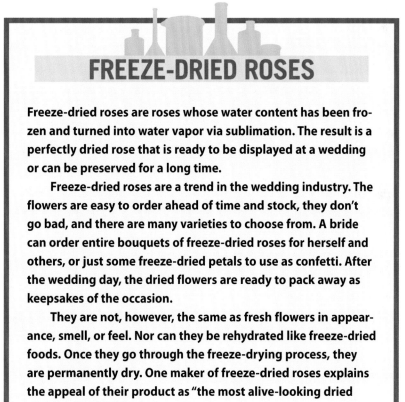

FREEZE-DRIED ROSES

Freeze-dried roses are roses whose water content has been frozen and turned into water vapor via sublimation. The result is a perfectly dried rose that is ready to be displayed at a wedding or can be preserved for a long time.

Freeze-dried roses are a trend in the wedding industry. The flowers are easy to order ahead of time and stock, they don't go bad, and there are many varieties to choose from. A bride can order entire bouquets of freeze-dried roses for herself and others, or just some freeze-dried petals to use as confetti. After the wedding day, the dried flowers are ready to pack away as keepsakes of the occasion.

They are not, however, the same as fresh flowers in appearance, smell, or feel. Nor can they be rehydrated like freeze-dried foods. Once they go through the freeze-drying process, they are permanently dry. One maker of freeze-dried roses explains the appeal of their product as "the most alive-looking dried roses available."[14]

MELTING

Recycling is the process of taking used materials, such as glass and plastic bottles, paper, and aluminum cans, and reprocessing them to make new products. One of the most common ways materials are recycled uses melting. Solids are melted into liquids, which are cleaned or processed as needed before being made into new things. Recycling of glass, plastic, and metal all take advantage of this phase change.

Glass

Glass is an amorphous solid made mostly of silica molecules (SiO_2), the main ingredient in sand. Glass has long been used to construct beverage and food containers because it is sturdy, transparent, and fairly easy to make.

When glass is recycled, it is first divided into its three common colors: clear, green, and brown. Colored glass has added ingredients that cannot be easily removed, so sorting is necessary before recycling. Next, the glass is broken into small pieces, cleaned, melted, and reshaped into new things.

These small pieces melt at lower temperatures than is needed to manufacture glass from raw materials. The phase change occurs when the molecules in the solid glass pieces gather enough energy to break out of their structure and flow as liquids. The exact amount of energy needed depends on the type of glass involved.

Partly because it takes less energy to recycle glass than to make new glass, glass recycling companies in the United States represent a $5.5 billion industry, with 65 glass recycling plants in 25 different states.[15] Likewise, recycled glass is identical to new glass. In this case, the conversion between solid and liquid states of matter does not affect the final quality of the product.

Plastic

Plastic is a synthetic material made largely of chains of molecules bonded together during complex chemical reactions. Most plastics are considered partly amorphous and partly crystalline solids. They come in many varieties and are commonly used in household products.

The plastics used to construct beverage containers are most often targeted for recycling, but the process gets complicated quickly. There are many different types of plastics, each containing chains of different molecules in different orders. Each type of plastic is designated with a number in a triangle, usually on the bottom of the container.

When plastics are recycled, each type of plastic must be processed by itself. Mixing different types of plastics is like trying to mix oil and water: It just doesn't work at the molecular level. Essentially, recycling plastic is like separating a long train into its individual train cars and then putting them all back together again to make a new train. This separation can occur by chemical or thermal (heat) means.

Chemical separation of the chains of molecules in plastics usually involves a phase change. The process uses chemical reactions to change the order of molecules in a plastic, sometimes producing a liquid, gas, or another solid.

Heat is also used to separate the chains of molecules in plastics physically. When plastics are heated, the molecules gather enough energy to break away from their chains and solid structures. Like chemical separation, melting can result in new liquids, gases, or other solids. These new liquids, gases, and solids are then used as raw ingredients to construct new plastic products.

Another type of plastic recycling doesn't involve a phase change at all. Instead, plastics are chopped into small pieces and pasted back together in new forms. Such "plastic lumber" can be used to construct park benches, porches, and playground equipment.

Because recycling plastic takes many forms, the plastic recycling industry is not as large as some other forms of recycling, but it is growing. There are six times more companies handling recycled plastics today than there were 20 years ago, and the market demand for recycled materials continues to grow.[16]

Aluminum

Aluminum is an element and is one of the most abundant metals on Earth. This soft, lightweight metal is often used in packaging to make beverage containers and foil. Recycling of aluminum is

RECYCLED CELL PHONES

By 2002, there were about 1 billion cell phones in use throughout the world. By 2005, experts estimated that about 500 million unused cell phones were stuck in drawers and closets for storage. According to experts at the United States Geological Survey (USGS), the earth science branch of the federal government, these discarded cell phones are a treasure trove of valuable metals waiting to be recycled.

While one particular cell phone doesn't have huge quantities of valuable metals, taken as a group, unused cell phones could be a huge source of rare, recyclable metals. This would add significantly to metals already recycled in the United States and perhaps alleviate pressure on mining for new metals.

At the moment, there are no programs or processes in place for recycling the materials that cell phones are made from. According to the USGS, less than one percent of the cell phones thrown away every year are actually recycled in some way. Like many of the parts in obsolete electronics, no one is quite sure what to do with them or how to make a profit in recycling. [17]

TABLE 9.1 CELL PHONE RECYCLING INFORMATION

METAL IN CELL PHONES	TOTAL WEIGHT OF METAL IN 500 MILLION UNUSED CELL PHONES	TOTAL VALUE
Copper	7,900 metric tons	$17 million
Silver	178 metric tons	$31 million
Gold	17 metric tons	$199 million
Platinum	0.18 metric tons	$3.9 million

one of the oldest, most cost-efficient forms of recycling practiced today.

Like glass recycling, the process of recycling aluminum is fairly simple. Previously used aluminum packaging is shredded into small solid pieces, which are then melted inside a furnace to produce a thick liquid. At this point, the molten aluminum is identical to raw aluminum being processed for the first time. It is reshaped and reprocessed to create new products and packaging.

Perhaps because of the simple process, making aluminum cans from recycled materials takes 95 percent less energy than it takes to make cans from raw materials. Because of this efficiency, billions of cans are recycled every year.[17] In addition, aluminum car parts, windows, doors, and appliances are also recycled regularly.

DEPOSITION

Deposition is used in industry to create very thin films of material on the surfaces of objects. This process, known as physical vapor deposition (PVD), takes specific gas molecules and changes them into solids that are deposited as coatings on the surface of objects. In some cases, the coatings are protective; in other cases, the coatings create a pleasing appearance.

Most people have likely never heard of the PVD process, but surely use PVD products. The general concept of putting a protective coating on a surface is not entirely unknown. Paint contains chemicals that deposit a protective layer on the surface of objects. Electroplating uses electricity to deposit a layer of metal on the surface of tableware, jewelry, and coins. The PVD process uses phase changes to deposit layers on the surface of objects.

One advantage of physical vapor deposition is its preciseness. Extremely thin layers, sometimes only a few atoms thick, can be applied to a surface. This deposition process is widely used in the manufacturing of semiconductors, the chip-like circuits used in many electronic devices.

Figure 9.3   This micro-chip has been coated using the PVD process. The coating provides protection for the information stored in the chip.

Semiconductors are ultra-thin, polished "wafers" often made of pure silicon, one of the most abundant elements on Earth. One of the first steps in making a semiconductor is to use deposition to coat the surface of the wafer. Depending on the intended use for the semiconductor, it can be coated with a variety of materials.

Physical vapor deposition is also used to add a clear coat to aluminum balloons and snack bags. The deposition of a specific film made from polyester on the outside of shiny, aluminum balloons gives the balloon added strength while the film remains transparent. The deposition of a similar polyester film on snack bags provides a solid barrier to gases and smells. This industrial phase change is not particularly glamorous or well-known, but it is used in many applications that consumers use in everyday products.

SUMMARY

How molecules move, behave, and are organized in nature is not always understood by scientists. With some understanding of the basic chemistry laws that govern the molecules, however, these states can be explained, predicted, and, often times, changed. By changing and controlling the state of matter of different things on Earth, humans have a lot to gain. Evidence of this concept can be seen in many of the products that are used in homes and industries throughout the world.

In the different stages of Earth's water cycle, water can change into a liquid, solid, or gas state, which results in the movement of water around the globe. Humans cause the states of matter to change, often to improve the conditions of their lives. Humans and other forms of life are dependent upon many changes in the states of matter.

PERIODIC TABLE OF THE ELEMENTS

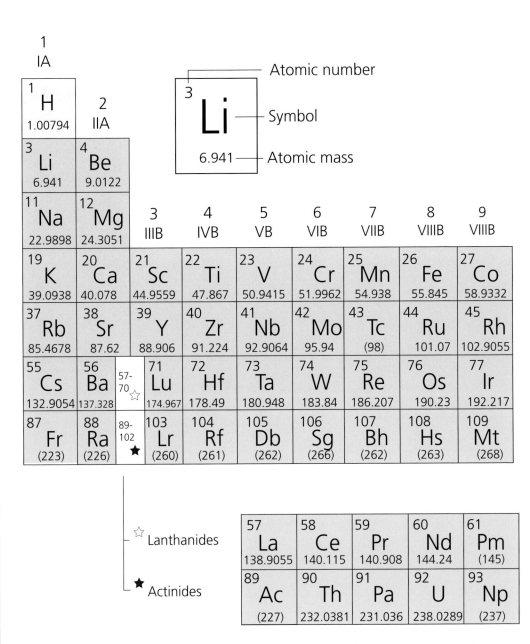

Numbers in parentheses are atomic mass numbers of most stable isotopes.

							18 VIIIA

Metals

Non-metals

Metalloids

			13 IIIA	14 IVA	15 VA	16 VIA	17 VIIA	2 He 4.0026
			5 B 10.81	6 C 12.011	7 N 14.0067	8 O 15.9994	9 F 18.9984	10 Ne 20.1798
10 VIIIB	11 IB	12 IIB	13 Al 26.9815	14 Si 28.0855	15 P 30.9738	16 S 32.067	17 Cl 35.4528	18 Ar 39.948
28 Ni 58.6934	29 Cu 63.546	30 Zn 65.409	31 Ga 69.723	32 Ge 72.61	33 As 74.9216	34 Se 78.96	35 Br 79.904	36 Kr 83.798
46 Pd 106.42	47 Ag 107.8682	48 Cd 112.412	49 In 114.818	50 Sn 118.711	51 Sb 121.760	52 Te 127.60	53 I 126.9045	54 Xe 131.29
78 Pt 195.08	79 Au 196.9655	80 Hg 200.59	81 Tl 204.3833	82 Pb 207.2	83 Bi 208.9804	84 Po (209)	85 At (210)	86 Rn (222)
110 Ds (271)	111 Rg (272)	112 Uub (277)						

62 Sm 150.36	63 Eu 151.966	64 Gd 157.25	65 Tb 158.9253	66 Dy 162.500	67 Ho 164.9303	68 Er 167.26	69 Tm 168.9342	70 Yb 173.04
94 Pu (244)	95 Am 243	96 Cm (247)	97 Bk (247)	98 Cf (251)	99 Es (252)	100 Fm (257)	101 Md (258)	102 No (259)

ELECTRON CONFIGURATIONS

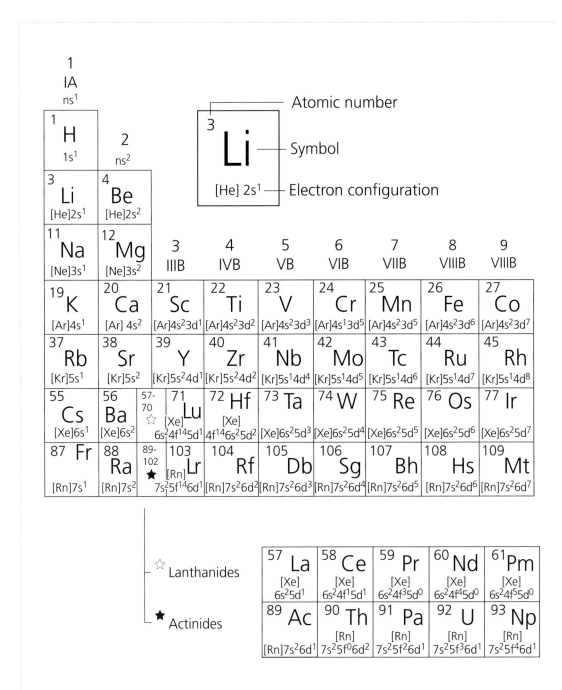

			13 IIIA ns^2np^1	14 IVA ns^2np^2	15 VA ns^2np^3	16 VIA ns^2np^4	17 VIIA ns^2np^5	18 VIIIA ns^2np^6
								2 He $1s^2$
			5 B $[He]2s^22p^1$	6 C $[He]2s^22p^2$	7 N $[He]2s^22p^3$	8 O $[He]2s^22p^4$	9 F $[He]2s^22p^5$	10 Ne $[He]2s^22p^6$
10 VIIIB	11 IB	12 IIB	13 Al $[Ne]3s^23p^1$	14 Si $[Ne]3s^23p^2$	15 P $[Ne]3s^23p^3$	16 S $[Ne]3s^23p^4$	17 Cl $[Ne]3s^23p^5$	18 Ar $[Ne]3s^23p^6$
28 Ni $[Ar]4s^23d^8$	29 Cu $[Ar]4s^13d^{10}$	30 Zn $[Ar]4s^23d^{10}$	31 Ga $[Ar]4s^24p^1$	32 Ge $[Ar]4s^24p^2$	33 As $[Ar]4s^24p^3$	34 Se $[Ar]4s^24p^4$	35 Br $[Ar]4s^24p^5$	36 Kr $[Ar]4s^24p^6$
46 Pd $[Kr]4d^{10}$	47 Ag $[Kr]5s^14d^{10}$	48 Cd $[Kr]5s^24d^{10}$	49 In $[Kr]5s^25p^1$	50 Sn $[Kr]5s^25p^2$	51 Sb $[Kr]5s^25p^3$	52 Te $[Kr]5s^25p^4$	53 I $[Kr]5s^25p^5$	54 Xe $[Kr]5s^25p^6$
78 Pt $[Xe]6s^15d^9$	79 Au $[Xe]6s^15d^{10}$	80 Hg $[Xe]6s^25d^{10}$	81 Tl $[Xe]6s^26p^1$	82 Pb $[Xe]6s^26p^2$	83 Bi $[Xe]6s^26p^3$	84 Po $[Xe]6s^26p^4$	85 At $[Xe]6s^26p^5$	86 Rn $[Xe]6s^26p^6$
110 Ds $[Rn]7s^16d^9$	111 Rg $[Rn]7s^16d^{10}$	112 Uub $[Rn]7s^26d^{10}$						

62 Sm [Xe] $6s^24f^65d^0$	63 Eu [Xe] $6s^24f^75d^0$	64 Gd [Xe] $6s^24f^75d^1$	65 Tb [Xe] $6s^24f^95d^0$	66 Dy [Xe] $6s^24f^{10}5d^0$	67 Ho [Xe] $6s^24f^{11}5d^0$	68 Er [Xe] $6s^24f^{12}5d^0$	69 Tm [Xe] $6s^24f^{13}5d^0$	70 Yb [Xe] $6s^24f^{14}5d^0$
94 Pu [Rn] $7s^25f^66d^0$	95 Am [Rn] $7s^25f^76d^0$	96 Cm [Rn] $7s^25f^76d^1$	97 Bk [Rn] $7s^25f^96d^0$	98 Cf [Rn] $7s^25f^{10}6d^0$	99 Es [Rn] $7s^25f^{11}6d^0$	100 Fm [Rn] $7s^25f^{12}6d^0$	101 Md [Rn] $7s^25f^{13}6d^0$	102 No [Rn] $7s^25f^{14}6d^1$

TABLE OF ATOMIC MASSES

ELEMENT	SYMBOL	ATOMIC NUMBER	ATOMIC MASS	ELEMENT	SYMBOL	ATOMIC NUMBER	ATOMIC MASS
Actinium	Ac	89	(227)	Francium	Fr	87	(223)
Aluminum	Al	13	26.9815	Gadolinium	Gd	64	157.25
Americium	Am	95	243	Gallium	Ga	31	69.723
Antimony	Sb	51	121.76	Germanium	Ge	32	72.61
Argon	Ar	18	39.948	Gold	Au	79	196.9655
Arsenic	As	33	74.9216	Hafnium	Hf	72	178.49
Astatine	At	85	(210)	Hassium	Hs	108	(263)
Barium	Ba	56	137.328	Helium	He	2	4.0026
Berkelium	Bk	97	(247)	Holmium	Ho	67	164.9303
Beryllium	Be	4	9.0122	Hydrogen	H	1	1.00794
Bismuth	Bi	83	208.9804	Indium	In	49	114.818
Bohrium	Bh	107	(262)	Iodine	I	53	126.9045
Boron	B	5	10.81	Iridium	Ir	77	192.217
Bromine	Br	35	79.904	Iron	Fe	26	55.845
Cadmium	Cd	48	112.412	Krypton	Kr	36	83.798
Calcium	Ca	20	40.078	Lanthanum	La	57	138.9055
Californium	Cf	98	(251)	Lawrencium	Lr	103	(260)
Carbon	C	6	12.011	Lead	Pb	82	207.2
Cerium	Ce	58	140.115	Lithium	Li	3	6.941
Cesium	Cs	55	132.9054	Lutetium	Lu	71	174.967
Chlorine	Cl	17	35.4528	Magnesium	Mg	12	24.3051
Chromium	Cr	24	51.9962	Manganese	Mn	25	54.938
Cobalt	Co	27	58.9332	Meitnerium	Mt	109	(268)
Copper	Cu	29	63.546	Mendelevium	Md	101	(258)
Curium	Cm	96	(247)	Mercury	Hg	80	200.59
Darmstadtium	Ds	110	(271)	Molybdenum	Mo	42	95.94
Dubnium	Db	105	(262)	Neodymium	Nd	60	144.24
Dysprosium	Dy	66	162.5	Neon	Ne	10	20.1798
Einsteinium	Es	99	(252)	Neptunium	Np	93	(237)
Erbium	Er	68	167.26	Nickel	Ni	28	58.6934
Europium	Eu	63	151.966	Niobium	Nb	41	92.9064
Fermium	Fm	100	(257)	Nitrogen	N	7	14.0067
Fluorine	F	9	18.9984	Nobelium	No	102	(259)

ELEMENT	SYMBOL	ATOMIC NUMBER	ATOMIC MASS	ELEMENT	SYMBOL	ATOMIC NUMBER	ATOMIC MASS
Osmium	Os	76	190.23	Silicon	Si	14	28.0855
Oxygen	O	8	15.9994	Silver	Ag	47	107.8682
Palladium	Pd	46	106.42	Sodium	Na	11	22.9898
Phosphorus	P	15	30.9738	Strontium	Sr	38	87.62
Platinum	Pt	78	195.08	Sulfur	S	16	32.067
Plutonium	Pu	94	(244)	Tantalum	Ta	73	180.948
Polonium	Po	84	(209)	Technetium	Tc	43	(98)
Potassium	K	19	39.0938	Tellurium	Te	52	127.6
Praseodymium	Pr	59	140.908	Terbium	Tb	65	158.9253
Promethium	Pm	61	(145)	Thallium	Tl	81	204.3833
Protactinium	Pa	91	231.036	Thorium	Th	90	232.0381
Radium	Ra	88	(226)	Thulium	Tm	69	168.9342
Radon	Rn	86	(222)	Tin	Sn	50	118.711
Rhenium	Re	75	186.207	Titanium	Ti	22	47.867
Rhodium	Rh	45	102.9055	Tungsten	W	74	183.84
Roentgenium	Rg	111	(272)	Ununbium	Uub	112	(277)
Rubidium	Rb	37	85.4678	Uranium	U	92	238.0289
Ruthenium	Ru	44	101.07	Vanadium	V	23	50.9415
Rutherfordium	Rf	104	(261)	Xenon	Xe	54	131.29
Samarium	Sm	62	150.36	Ytterbium	Yb	70	173.04
Scandium	Sc	21	44.9559	Yttrium	Y	39	88.906
Seaborgium	Sg	106	(266)	Zinc	Zn	30	65.409
Selenium	Se	34	78.96	Zirconium	Zr	40	91.224

NOTES

1   "Climate of 2005: Summary of Hurricane Katrina." NOAA
    Satellite and Information Service, National Climatic Data
    Center Web Site. Available online. URL: http://www.ncdc.
    noaa.gov/oa/climate/research/2005/katrina.html. Accessed
    October 25, 2006.

2   R.D. Knabb, J.R Rhome, and D.P. Brown. "Tropical Cycline
    Report: Hurricane Katrina." National Hurricane Center Web
    Site. Available online. URL: http://www.nhc.noaa.gov/pdf/
    TCR-AL122005_Katrina.pdf. Accessed December 20, 2005.

3   "Evaporation." USGS Water Science Basics, USGS Web Site.
    Available online. URL: http://ga.water.usgs.gov/edu/
    watercycleevaporation.html. Accessed November 6, 2006.

4   "The Water Cycle: Snowmelt Runoff to Streams." USGS
    Water Science Basics, USGS Web Site. Available online.
    URL:http://ga.water.usgs.gov/edu/watercyclesnowmelt.html.
    Accessed November 14, 2006.

5   "Global Ice Melt Accelerating." Worldwatch Institute
    Vital Signs Online. Worldwatch Institute Web Site. Avail-
    able online. URL: http://www.worldwatch.org/node/4266.
    Accessed November 14, 2006.

6   "Water Storage in Ice and Snow." USGS Water Science Basics,
    USGS Web Site. Available online. URL: http://ga.water.usgs.
    gov/edu/watercycleice.html. Accessed November 11, 2006.

7   "A Tour of the Life of a Glacier." National Snow and Ice Data
    Center Web Site. Available online. URL: http://nsidc.org/
    glaciers/story/. Accessed November 16, 2006.

8   "The Water Cycle: Sublimation." USGS Water Science Basics,
    USGS Web Site. Available online. URL: http://ga.water.usgs.
    gov/edu/watercyclesublimation.html. Accessed on Novem-
    ber 16, 2006.

9   Ian Guch, *The Complete Idiot's Guide to Chemistry.* New York:
    Alpha Books. 2003, p.179.

10 Dr. Timothy Eastman, "Perspective on Plasmas." NASA
    GSFC Space Physics Data Facility, Plasmas International

Web Site. Available online. URL: http://www.plasmas. org/basics.htm. Accessed November 17, 2006.

11   "Particulate." Wikipedia: The Free Encyclopedia Web Site. Available online. URL: http://en.wikipedia.org/wiki/ Particulate. Accessed November 18, 2006.

12   Paul Doherty, and Linda Shore. "Better Hair Through Chemistry." Exploratorium Web Site. Available online. URL: http://www.exploratorium.edu/exploring/hair/ hair_activity.html. Accessed November 18, 2006.

13   "Steam Turbine." Wikipedia: The Free Encyclopedia Web Site. Available online. URL: http://en.wikipedia.org/wiki/ Steam_turbine. Accessed November 18, 2006.

14   "About Rose City Freeze Dry." Rose City Freeze Dry Web Site. Available online. URL: http://www.rosecityfreezedry. com/about.shtml. Accessed November 18, 2006.

15   "FAQs." Glass Packaging Institute. Available online. URL: http://www.gpi.org/recycling/faq/. Accessed November 19, 2006.

16   "State of Plastic Recycling." The American Plastics Council Web Site. Available online. URL: http://www. plasticsresource.com/s_plasticsresource/sec.asp? TRACKID=&CID=155&DID=260. Accessed November 19, 2006.

17   Daniel E. Sullivan, "Recycled Cell Phones: A Treasure Trove of Valuable Metals." United States Geological Survey Web Site. Available online. URL: http://pubs.usgs.gov/ fs/2006/3097/fs2006–3097.pdf. Accessed November 19, 2006.

18   "Facts About Aluminum Recycling." Earth 911 Web Site. Available online. URL: http://www.earth911.org/master. asp?s=lib&a=aluminum/facts.asp. Accessed November 19, 2006.

GLOSSARY

Absolute zero The temperature at which all molecular motion stops and there is no thermal energy left in a substance.

Aerosol A tiny piece of solid or liquid suspended in a gas.

Amorphous solid A solid held together by unpredictable bonds and forces.

Apocrine sweat glands Glands that produce fatty, odor-heavy liquids in the armpits and around the genital areas of humans.

Atom The smallest part of an element that still maintains the properties of that element.

Boiling point The temperature at which a liquid changes to a gas.

Bose-Einstein condensate (BEC) A super-cold, super-slow moving clump of atoms; considered a unique state of matter by some scientists.

Chemical bond The force created when electrons are gained, lost, or shared to create a molecule of two or more atoms.

Chemical formulas Short way to show the elements that make up a molecule of a substance.

Chemical reaction When substances react with one another to form new substances.

Close-packed structure A solid in which each atom is as close to the next atom as possible.

Condensation The process in which a gas changes into a liquid.

Covalent bond Bond formed when atoms share electrons.

Crystalline solid A solid whose particles are organized in definite geometric patterns.

Deposition The process by which a gas changes into a solid.

Dipole A molecule having both a negatively and positively charged area, separated in space.

Dipole-dipole interactions A type of intermolecular force that occurs when the positively charged end of one molecule is attracted to the negatively charged end of another molecule.

Dispersion force A type of intermolecular force that occurs when molecules become temporarily charged, either positively or negatively, and become attracted to each other.

Eccrine sweat glands Glands that produce and release sweat to regulate the temperature of the body.

Electric field The space surrounding a charged particle that exerts a force on other particles.

Electronegative The more electronegative something is, the more readily it attracts electrons.

Electrostatic force The force that holds oppositely charged particles together.

Electrons Negatively charged, subatomic particles inside the atom; they allow one atom to bond with another atom.

Element The most basic substances in the universe; they cannot be broken down to create different things.

Endothermic reaction A reaction that requires heat to occur.

Evaporation The process by which a liquid changes into a gas.

Exothermic reaction A reaction that releases heat.

Freezing point The temperature at which a liquid changes into a solid. It is the same temperature as the melting point of the solid.

Gland An organ that creates and releases special substances in the human body, including hormones and other liquids.

Hydrogen bond A type of dipole-dipole interaction that occurs when a hydrogen atom is attracted to an atom in another molecule.

Ideal gas law The equation for an ideal gas that shows the relationship between the product of the pressure and volume to the product of the temperature and amount of gas molecules written as $PV = nRT$.

Intermolecular force A force between two or more molecules; tends to be weaker than the force of a chemical bond.

Ionic bond   When one atom gives an electron to another atom.

Ionic solid   A solid held together by ionic bonds.

Kinetic energy   The energy of motion.

Liquid crystals   A substance between a liquid and a solid.

Magnetic field   A substance that exerts a force on a moving, charged particle.

Matter   Anything that takes up space.

Melting   The process by which a solid changes into a liquid.

Melting point   The temperature at which a solid becomes a liquid, the same as the freezing point.

Metallic bond   Bond formed when two metal atoms share electrons.

Metallic solid   A solid held together by metallic bonds.

Molecular solid   A solid held together by intermolecular forces.

Molecule   Particle produced when two or more atoms are bonded together by sharing electrons.

Neutrons   Neutrally charged, subatomic particles.

Nucleus   Densely packed central region of an atom that consists of positively charged particles called protons and neutral particles called neutrons.

Octet rule   The tendency of atoms to be stable with eight electrons in their outermost energy level.

Orbitals   Energy levels where electrons reside in an atom.

Periodic table   An organized chart of the elements.

Phase change   A substance changes its form, or state of matter.

Phase diagram   Shows the state of matter of a given material under all possible temperatures and pressures.

Plasma   An ionized gas; widely considered to be the fourth state of matter.

Pressure   The amount of force exerted by atoms or molecules on a given space.

Property　A characteristic behavior of a chemical substance.

Protons　Positively charged, subatomic particles inside the atom.

Shape　Measurable dimensions.

State of matter　Determines how molecules move, behave, and occupy a space. The three main states of matter are solids, liquids, and gases.

Steam engines　Devices that boil liquid water to produce gaseous steam to drive moving parts, and condense it back into liquid to be boiled again.

Subatomic particles　Particles inside an atom; includes protons, neutrons, and electrons.

Sublimation　The process of changing a solid into a gas.

Supercritical fluids　Liquids that don't behave like normal liquids and instead have properties of both liquids and gases.

Superfluid　A liquid that will flow endlessly when placed in a closed loop.

Supersolid　A superfluid with the crystal-like structure of a traditional solid.

Temperature　A measurement of the average kinetic energy of a group of particles.

Triple point　The temperature and pressure at which the solid, liquid, and gaseous forms of one type of matter are all equally possible.

Vacuum　A space empty of matter.

Volume　Occupation of a defined amount of space.

Water cycle　Describes the movement of water on, above, and below the surface of the Earth.

BIBLIOGRAPHY

Bloomfield, Louis A. *How Things Work: The Physics of Everyday Life*. New York: John Wiley & Sons, 1997.

Eastman, Dr. Timothy. "Perspective on Plasmas." NASA GSFC Space Physics Data Facility, Plasmas International Web Site. Available online. URL: http://www.plasmas.org/. Accessed November 17, 2006.

Guch, Ian. *The Complete Idiot's Guide to Chemistry*. New York: Alpha Books, 2003.

Moore, John T. *Chemistry for Dummies*. New York: Wiley Publishing, 2003.

Moore, John T., *Chemistry Made Simple*. New York: Broadway Books, 2004.

FURTHER READING

Baldwin, Carol. *States of Matter.* Chicago: Raintree Publishing, July 2005.

Broecker, Wallace S. *How to Build a Habitable Planet.* New York: Trustees of Columbia University, 1998.

Gardner, Robert. *Science Projects about Solids, Liquids, and Gases.* Enslow Publishers, Berkeley Heights, NJ. July 2000.

Gore, Al. *An Inconvenient Truth: The Planetary Emergency of Global Warming and What We Can Do About It.* New York: Rodale Books, May 2006.

Johnson, Rebecca L. *Atomic Structure.* Breckenridge, CO: Twenty-First Century Books, October 2007.

Kras, Sarah Louise. *The Steam Engine.* New York: Chelsea House Publishing, July 2003.

Palser, Barb. *Hurricane Katrina: Aftermath of a Disaster.* Minnesota: Compass Point Books, August 2006.

Saunders, Nigel. *Tungsten and the Elements of Groups 3 to 7.* Chicago: Heinemann, February 2004.

West, Krista. *Chemistry Matters! Chemical Reactions.* London: Brown Reference Group, 2007.

White, Katherine. *Mendeleyev and the Periodic Table.* New York: Rosen Publishing, 2005.

Web Sites

Environmental Protection Agency
Recycle City
http://www.epa.gov/recyclecity/

Administered by the Environmental Protection Agency (EPA), this interactive site features "Recycle City," a fictional town that serves as a learning tool related to recycling and environmental awareness.

National Center for Atmospheric Research
University Corporation for Atmospheric Research
Kids Crossing: Hurricanes
http://eo.ucar.edu/kids/dangerwx/hurricane1.htm

This site provides a detailed overview of the causes and effects of hurricanes and other types of severe weather. Students can navigate other links for more information about weather, the atmosphere, and the environment.

National Snow and Ice Data Center
University of Colorado Cooperative Institute for Research in Environmental Sciences
http://nsidc.org/

Find the latest research about the Earth's polar environments and the impact of climate change on polar ice caps. Site provides links to additional data centers and NSIDC publications.

Perspective on Plasmas
Plasmas International
NASA GSFC Space Physics Data Facility
http://www.plasmas.org/

This site offers comprehensive information on plasma, the fourth state of matter. Students, educators, and the public can find out about the discovery of plasma, its components, and its scientific and practical uses.

TryScience!
New York Hall of Science, Association of Science Technology Centers, IBM
http://www.tryscience.org/

An online gateway for students, teachers, and scientists, this site promotes the value of science education and importance of science centers. Visitors can learn about science-related news, view live web cams, conduct online experiments, and find links to a plethora of science centers around the world.

United States Geological Survey
Water Science for Schools: The Water Cycle
http://ga.water.usgs.gov/edu/watercycle.html

Understand the science of water via this site administered by the U.S. Geological Survey. Comprehensive text and interactive tools inform students (and parents) of the water cycle and other water-related data.

PHOTO CREDITS

INDEX

ABOUT THE AUTHOR

Chemistry was never an easy topic for science writer **KRISTA WEST**. Only after years of studying chemistry in life science and earth science did she realize (and appreciate) its power. Today, she writes young adult chemistry books on topics as diverse as states of matter, chemical reactions, and the properties of metals. Krista holds master's degrees in Earth Science and Journalism, both from Columbia University in New York. She lives in Fairbanks, Alaska with her husband and two sons.